Advance Praise for *Dark F...*

"Pick up a hammer. Hit yourself in ... ...ay will feel like as the action overwhel... ... ...night. Jeffrey Leever's got himself a big, bold winn...
— Shane Gericke, author of the bestseller *Cut to the Bone*

"Fast-paced, heart-pounding suspense. *Dark Friday* combines the thrills of a young James Patterson with the chills of Stephen King."
— Troy Cook, *The One Minute Assassin*

"A new talent to be reckoned with."
— *Midwest Book Review*

"Leever can clearly write and he knows how to put together a gripping nail-biter of a thriller."
— Norm Goldman, Bookpleasures.com

"A first-time author worth watching—and reading."
— Rose & Thorn

"Well-paced, with enough intrigue and mystery to hold you spell-bound."
— Bookideas.com

"A slam-bang opening, with taut prose, and plenty of mystery."
— Donald Maass, *Writing the Breakout Novel*

"Will keep you flipping the pages long into the night."
— The American Chronicle

"Jeffrey Leever is a talented writer who I am sure will have a great career as an author."
— Hon. Bill Owens, former two-term governor of Colorado

"Quick, tight, fast, and frightening, Leever is the type of writer who knows how to pace a novel."
— Phillip Tomasso III, *Adverse Impact*

"One that deserves your attention."
— AuthorsDen.com

DARK FRIDAY

DARK FRIDAY

JEFFREY LEEVER

CAPITAL CRIME PRESS
FORT COLLINS, COLORADO

Copyright © 2007 by Jeffrey Leever

First edition published in the United States by Capital Crime Press. Printed in Canada.

Capital Crime Press is a registered trademark.

Library of Congress Catalog Card Number: 2007927721
ISBN: 9780977627639

www.capitalcrimepress.com

Kudos: Jeff Dunn, Jon Woodhams, Adam Palmer, Alex Cole, Troy Cook, Lori Lacefield, Marjorie Bayes, Su Wright, Ellen O'Connell, Apple Inc., and the real residents of Jasonville.

Über-Kudos: Ellen Larson, Anita Beery, Pam Getchell, and webmaster maestro Matt Rader.

For Erin.

"Write the story you have."

Thanks.

one

"Unbelievable!" screamed Police Chief Bertrand Rix. His car flew around the corner of Sixth and Sycamore, tires screeching through the neighborhood, just as another homicide report came over the radio.

Another brutal attack. Same M.O. This one even closer.

Un...be...lievable. The word didn't make it to his lips this time.

A figure burst into his path. Male, dark hair, running through the night super-quick, trying to cut across the street in front of Rix's car. Rix hammered his foot on the brake.

His tires shrieked again and Rix felt the impact. The car clipped the runner, launching him into the windshield. Rix heard the crackle and saw the glass spiderweb appear, then lost view of the body as it thumped across his roof.

The cruiser skidded to a stop. Had he just hit a suspect? A witness? Rix slammed the gearshift into park and reached for the door.

What the—? In the rearview mirror, Rix saw something round slide off the trunk. He opened the door and saw the runner now lying on the pavement.

Somehow the guy got up and started running again.

Rix was out of the car in a split-second. "Stop!"

The guy, who by all rights should've been dead, didn't stop.

"This is Police Chief Rix! You need medical attention!"
No response.

The injured sprinter ran with a limp but was still fast.

Rix glanced at the pavement and saw blood. He looked closer and realized what had fallen off his cruiser.

The guy was getting away, but Rix hesitated. A strange piece of plastic lay on the ground, like a black mirror in the darkness. Rix stared hard.

It was a paintball mask, smack in the middle of Sycamore Street, cracked and splattered with blood. The thing had disproportionately large goggled eyes, two eerie batlike slits for a nose, and no mouth. Along the cheeks were vertical, scarlike slashes. If The Fly and Darth Vader had spawned offspring, it might look like...like what he was seeing now.

Rix's mind was pounding. All the gruesome reports flying over the radio tonight—three, four, maybe more, only minutes apart, *someone in a mask* attacking people—this was no small-town prank.

He ripped his gun from its holster and ran in pursuit. "You're under arrest!" he shouted at the fleeing runner, not really expecting a response.

In twenty years on the job, he'd never once needed to say that phrase with his gun drawn. Then again, he'd never chased a homicide suspect before.

Rix saw the guy heading toward the town graveyard and felt ill inside.

FOUR BLOCKS AWAY HOPE REDMOND RAN AND CRIED, HER LETTER jacket torn, her blond hair damp.

Oh, God help me. Somebody. Anybody.

She came around a bush and turned up the block. *Houses. Dark.* She touched her shoulder, then the side of her face. *Blood.*

Her stomach felt queasy, her heart pounding.

Is he still coming?

She saw a light and ran toward the house.

The front porch was only steps away. She'd break in if she had to.

Hope was almost there when someone grabbed her arm. She screamed.

She couldn't rip free.

"Let *go*! Get away from me!" She lunged toward the door. "Help!"

"Hope?" It was a voice she recognized. "How the... what *happened*?"

She turned and the grip loosened.

"Hope, it's me, Casey." He let go and put his hands up. "Calm down! What's going on?"

Casey...Casey Wood. Yes, she knew who he was, but—

"Why did you grab me?" she said. "Wh-what are you doing out here?"

"Hope, it's okay. Let me help you." He tried to touch her again.

She took a step away, toward the house, still staring.

No knife. No mask. No blood.

Could it still be *him*?

RIX STEPPED INTO THE WEEDS AT THE EDGE OF THE CEMETERY and spoke into his radio, "I'm in pursuit. Lebanon Cemetery!"

He scanned the tombstones, the crosses and hearts standing ominously pale in the moonlight. Half a football field ahead, he saw the figure running diagonally across the graveyard.

He crouched and headed in, trying to be quick, yet cautious. The suspect fled to the east, and Rix thought about taking a shot. He raised his gun, but the figure darted behind a headstone.

Punk.

Rix ran, gun still raised, though he knew it was unwise to risk a shot. Not yet anyway. Not with the bloodbath his town had already seen tonight. Lots of ricochet potential in a dark graveyard.

He gained on the suspect, who now jogged like he was either tiring or scheming. The suspect slipped past some trees and Rix lost him entirely. He hurried ahead, easing up to the trees, just a few yards from where the suspect had disappeared. He paused to listen. *Nothing.*

Trees swayed in the wind. A car traveled off in the distance. No crunching of leaves. No breathing. No footsteps. Nothing but night.

Rix surveyed the graveyard. The silence was starting to bother him. *Where was his backup?*

As chief of a seven-man force, Rix knew there were certain limitations. He just never counted on a solo chase through a backdrop of human decay, in pursuit of someone suspected of horrific murders all over town.

To his far right—almost behind him—Rix thought he saw something move. He spun around. Movement a few rows down. Rix crept ahead. The pursuit had led him almost the entire distance across Lebanon Cemetery.

He heard a loud crash ahead of him.

What was—? Rix burst toward the sound, gun pointed with precision. His heart raced so fast it felt like he'd slammed an entire pot of coffee back at the station. He cleared a row of tombstones and stopped dead in his tracks.

Rix found himself in front of the lone full-scale mausoleum in the entire cemetery: Tyre's Tomb. The entrance door had been forced open.

He scanned the graveyard, then gazed slowly back toward the open door.

Rix couldn't remember exactly who was buried in Tyre's Tomb, but the story went that years ago, Family Tyre had insisted on something special for a loved one. Were they Catholic? He couldn't recall. Obviously they'd had the means.

He shined his flashlight inside but saw no one.

The open door dared him to make a move. Rix took a step closer. He held his gun and flashlight, hands crisscrossed, both pointed at the dark entrance. Rix was tired of running. He knew he needed to end this right now. Rix evaluated the area for ambush potential. A dirt road separated the border of the cemetery from a cornfield. Rix hoped the guy hadn't been far enough ahead to make it into the field, that the open mausoleum door wasn't a ruse. The corn was tall and could've hidden anyone well. But there was no movement, and in the moonlight, Rix couldn't make out any footprints in the dirt.

He focused back on the open tomb. He sensed that if he went in, he had a much greater chance of assuming permanent cemetery temperature. But it was either that or be a coward, and cowards and police chiefs weren't one and the same in his book.

A bead of sweat trickled down his forehead and stopped at his eyebrow. He moved forward, just inside the doorway. Rix heard a noise, and panned the area with the flashlight, which revealed nothing. He took one more step in, then hesitated.

He heard a sudden rush *behind* him and a huge force slammed into his back. Both the flashlight and gun went flying.

Rix felt a sharp pain, then another. He fell toward the tomb's floor. He knew he was being stabbed.

Rix roared in agony.

His assailant screamed back with rage.

"WHERE DID YOU COME FROM?" HOPE STAMMERED.

"I was over at Ashley's." Casey pointed down the street, the opposite direction from where she'd fled. "You know Ashley...we're all in the same history class."

Hope looked toward the houses, still wary. Someone was

trying to kill her; Casey had been out walking around.

"Were you in an accident? A fight?" He held out his hand.

Hope fought back tears. "Someone...just...tried..."

"Hope—"

"...to *stab* me."

After she spoke the words, Casey did something that bothered her.

He didn't say anything.

two

THE MOONLIGHT CAME THROUGH TOMMIE MOORER'S WINDOW blinds just right, making a jagged pattern on his Colts bedspread. It was time.

Tommie knew the hour was finally past midnight. His older brother, Van, had taught him about sneaking out—before Van got sent away. Tommie slipped out his window and slid down the maple tree in his front yard.

He headed up Hoosier Way, straight toward the highway to Lake Lenape.

"You keep the hell away from that lake at night!" their mother had once shrieked.

"We're not gonna keep the hell away, bro," Van had whispered when they were alone. "We're gonna *raise* some hell."

Van was so cool. Van didn't care.

Tommie came to the section of Hoosier that didn't have streetlights. He liked the dark. Tommie was a man of the night, like Van. Here he always looked more closely at the houses, *in* the houses. One time he'd seen a naked woman talking on the telephone. She'd been wrapped in a towel, but he hadn't told his friends that part.

Once he started acting like Van, everyone thought he was cool, too. Maybe the coolest kid in seventh grade.

He counted only three houses with lights on.

Tommie crept ahead, alert for something—a dog barking, a porch light coming on, or someone yelling—that might make him need to run. But he had a secret. He liked to run. Running free through the night in the street. Wind in his hair.

"This is *our* world, Tommie," Van had said.

Leaves rustled behind him. A train blew its horn off in the distance. A "For Sale By Owner" sign rattled in the breeze.

Tommie stopped at one of the houses that had lights on inside. He peered in through the window, but didn't see any people. Just a room with one of those huge arcade games in it. Pac-Man. He'd never played one of the big arcade games, but knew Pac-Man 'cause he'd played it on GameCube. He laughed at the picture painted on the side of the game—ghosts chasing a little yellow eating machine. Tommie turned away and walked past the house, gazing down the street.

He was the ghost.

Tommie jogged a few blocks until he got to Uncle Ned's place. Ned was his goofy relative from his mom's side. And of all the tricks Van had taught Tommie, the one he was about to pull was his favorite.

Uncle Ned had crap piled everywhere, making his property look like a cross between a yard sale and the town dump, plus two trailers, a tractor, a shed, and some old cars. Tommie approached the shed, reached above the door and found the key in the same place as always. He eased inside and crept out with Uncle Ned's moped.

Tommie snuck a glance over to the main trailer, where he knew Uncle Ned was sleeping like a hibernating grizzly. He waited a moment, like always, just to be sure.

He walked the moped quietly away from the shed. When he was out of view from the trailer, he hopped on and peddled.

When he passed the sign for Highway 48 West, he chuckled and turned the key.

CASEY COULDN'T SEEM TO GIVE A SINGLE WORD IN RESPONSE. For a moment Hope thought about running again.

The front porch light came on. A gray-haired woman wearing a robe opened the door and leaned out. "What are you kids doing out here?"

Hope couldn't speak. She kept staring at Casey. Was he reaching in his pocket?

He turned to the woman, a stunned expression on his face. "Call an ambulance and the police, and let her come inside until they arrive."

Hope looked into Casey's eyes. She realized he wasn't the one.

The woman gasped.

"And lock the doors."

TOMMIE SMILED AS THE BREEZE SMACKED AGAINST HIS FACE. He gripped the handlebars tighter and accelerated up the highway. The pavement was still a little slick from the rain earlier, but he didn't care. There were no cars in sight.

He loved the thrill he was feeling. Something inside him had come alive. Tommie laughed.

"All I got is a moped, moped, moped," he sang.

The wind made the moisture in Tommie's eyes feel cold. His hair blew back and his jacket fluttered like a parachute. He was almost to Lake Lenape.

Without a doubt he was the coolest kid in seventh grade. But man did he miss his brother. Van should be here. Van would laugh with him.

Tommie killed the engine and coasted, listening. He searched for campers, parked RVs, anything. In the summer there were always tents. Tents were the best. "Never know what you'll find," Van once told him with a wink.

He ditched the moped behind some bushes and waited there a moment.

Tommie breathed in, inhaling the lake's mixture of fish, algae, and skanky mud. He remembered tasting it once—a flavor like bad oysters marinated in toilet water—when Van had rolled him in an inner tube along the shore and the tube tipped.

Nothing. No one.

Tommie crept along Lenape's long shoreline, searching for anyone up to anything. He had to go slowly without a flashlight, but it was more fun that way.

He made it about halfway around the lake and was thinking about skipping the rest. Everything was dark and quiet. He stopped and stood on the bank of the lake, staring out.

He remembered fishing as a kid near this spot, his bobber going under for the first time when he was seven. His dad had raced around the lake to help, while Tommie cried out and tried to keep the fish from getting off the hook. A bluegill. The fishing trip was one of the last things he could remember his family doing together. Van got yelled at a lot on that trip.

Tommie picked up a rock and threw it into the water. He frowned, picked up another rock, and threw it farther. He picked up a third and heaved as hard as he could, the splash easily clearing his last throw.

He watched the ripples in the moonlight, spreading toward the far bank, and that's when he saw it.

Somebody approaching the lake.

Tommie moved quickly through the bushes and trees, toward the person, trying to get a closer look. He came to a patch of thick weeds and lost sight of the figure for a moment. He heard a splash.

Did someone jump in the water? He remembered Van's story about skinny-dippers. Maybe more people would follow this one in. Maybe girls.

Everything was quiet.

He peeked out at the water and saw no one. The splash had been too loud to be someone casting out a fishing line. *Where did that come from?*

Tommie froze.

He was maybe twenty feet from a tall person standing on the shore, staring out at Lake Lenape. Tommie was to the side of him so he couldn't make out a face.

The way the figure stood made Tommie nervous. Something had disturbed the water, but the figure stood in the same place. What was going on?

The lake was now totally calm. Then a cloud came between the moonlight and the lake, making everything darker. Tommie realized how far he was from the moped. *Not fun anymore.* He was about to make a break for it. He took a few steps, thinking he could clear a nearby bush and then go, trying to be as silent as he could.

The figure made a sudden turn in Tommie's direction. *No.* Tommie made a quick decision to lunge forward, toward a patch of weeds.

The figure took a couple steps toward him, then paused. Tommie didn't like this one bit.

Bad, bad, bad. He held his breath and watched. He tried to be still and hope the noise he'd made would get mistaken for a rabbit or something. If the figure came any closer, Tommie would have to run.

A foot kicked the weeds next to Tommie. Pieces of brush got in his eyes. Tommie muffled a gasp and tried to pull his legs in tight.

Everything got quiet.

Be still.

Tommie put his head to the ground and tried to make his body even smaller.

Silence.

Long.

Longer.

Tommie thought he heard a rumble in the sky. He didn't

like being the one who was scared. Scared wasn't cool. Slowly, he looked up.

Still there.

The moon came back out of the clouds. He closed one eye to get a better view through the branches. Tommie listened for something that might give him a chance. Someone driving by. Drunk campers. Park rangers. Anything to change the situation.

Nothing came.

The way the moonlight created shadows through the trees and brush, Tommie still couldn't make out a face. Sandburs and pebbles were poking at his shins, but he didn't dare shift.

Then the figure moved and Tommie caught a glimpse. He didn't want to believe it.

Finally, the guy turned to leave. Tommie let out a breath. The guy walked away slowly.

After a long, long minute, Tommie heard a car start.

He headed for the moped as fast as he could. He wouldn't be bragging to his friends about anything this time.

Rix's momentum carried him crashing into a coffin. His attacker slipped and Rix seized the opportunity. He couldn't see very well, but he threw an elbow where he thought his attacker's face would be.

Rix saw where his gun landed. The suspect was closer to it. They both went for it, but the suspect kicked it away. Rix lunged at him, slamming him against the stone wall. They locked arms and shoved each other along the wall until getting caught on the door, which, Rix realized, opened inward. He loosened his grip, trying to push the guy out of the tomb. The suspect planted his foot between the open door and the wall. Rix let out a roar and tried to throw the guy, but his wounded shoulder wouldn't cooperate.

The suspect suddenly kicked the door shut with his foot.

"No!" Rix still had the guy by the arm and tried to pull him down. Instead, Rix got tagged with an incredibly hard blow to his jaw. He dropped like a brick.

In a haze, Rix groped around in the total darkness.

He was closed inside Tyre's Tomb with a missing gun, a smashed flashlight, a knife, and at least one corpse.

And the suspect.

Which way is out?

He heard a sound and groggily tried to face it. He reached out one hand, ready for anything.

Rix clambered for the door. He couldn't believe the guy had shut them in.

Damn! Rix had terrible, sharp pain in his shoulder. He reached back and felt the warm, wet oozing of his own blood.

He retreated a step, then attempted to be still. He exhaled slowly and tried to think.

Rix waited. He discerned movement. It seemed to pass quickly, but then came by again.

Closer.

His instincts told him to be still. Everything was too quiet.

Was the guy blocking the exit, waiting with his knife?

Rix had a sick feeling like a cornered animal. His back and shoulder throbbed with searing pain.

Then came rage; he couldn't stop it. He didn't plan on dying in a graveyard.

He waited for another sound. He heard one, his own foot bumping something. Something solid. A rock? He wasn't sure what it was, but he'd find a use for it. Ever-so-quietly, he picked it up and waited.

More movement.

Rix threw the rock as hard as he could toward the sound, then attacked. He guessed well and got his arms around the figure, tackling him savagely. He heard the wind going out of the suspect and a weak groan. Rix pounded on him a few times just to be safe.

He dragged his subdued attacker along the mausoleum's floor with one hand, groping with the other. He found a wall, and, eventually, the door. He pulled it open.

The face-down suspect didn't seem too lively now. Rix reached to his belt, found his handcuffs, and snapped them over the guy's wrists. He pulled the assailant out of Tyre's Tomb and onto the grass.

Rix flipped the suspect over and in the moonlight saw a young face, one he recognized instantly, staring back. Rix's jaw dropped.

This kid was responsible for attacking people all over town?

A strange thought came to Rix and for a second he felt ashamed. He thought of evil. The forms it takes. And how no one—not even in Jasonville, Indiana—was immune to it.

Then he looked up through the fog and waved toward his finally-arriving backup.

three

EXCERPT FROM AN ARTICLE BY *INDIANAPOLIS TRIBUNE* INVESTIGATIVE WRITER KEVIN GIBSON

JASONVILLE, Ind.—Four hours south of Gary, Indiana, the occasional murder capital of the U.S., you'll find a little town called Jasonville. Among the pines, sycamores, and dormant spring peepers lies a tiny, inconspicuous community that takes all of five minutes to drive through. With one high school, one post office, a lone Subway (but no McDonald's), and a single, struggling movie theater, Jasonville appears to be bona fide Smalltown, USA.

Look around. Talk to the people. Breathe the air. The picture grows clear: This could be your town.

Jasonville (pop. 2,500) appears on most maps, but if you blink you may miss it. Along the Eel River, down Highway 59 off Interstate 70, most drivers are more likely to notice a box turtle on the road than the sign for Jasonville.

This isn't the most frequented of Indiana communities, and in light of recent events that's probably best: Five murders, two attempted murders—including an attack on the Chief of Police—all on the same rainy October night. If the town's population wasn't too small to qualify on a per capita basis, Jasonville just might give Gary a run for its money.

When the Governor of Indiana and the President

of the United States are both fielding questions about your town, you know you've hit the big time. Jasonville seems destined to go down in history as a place of infamy.

But longtime residents like LeAnne Craver are having none of it.

"Don't judge this place by what's happened," says Craver, a bartender and mother of two, including a teenage son who was a classmate of the victims. "This isn't the hellhole they're making it out to be."

Hellhole or not, many in town admit the national attention Jasonville is receiving is, in part, deserved.

Nevertheless, when Craver declares, "We're normal, God-fearing people. Good, kind citizens live here," one tends to believe her.

Craver personifies the typical Jasonville resident. Age 46 and possessing a college degree, she works part-time at Randall's Bar & Grill, one of a pair of after-hours spots in Jasonville. "It's where you get to know folks," she says.

Buster Randall—the bar's owner—still has a 1981 Indiana State Final Four banner on the wall and swears Larry Bird has one more championship left in him. Randall doesn't hesitate when asked about the state of the community. "You can get a feel for the people here. This isn't a community of killers." Randall's words sound practiced, like he's been rehearsing a sound bite, but the intensity with which he utters them is convincing. "We're honest and hardworking. It's quiet mostly, sometimes even a little boring. That's what you find when you look closely."

Standing next to her boss, Craver adds: "At least that's what you'd find if you visited any other time."

— AS POSTED ONLINE

AUGUST: TWO MONTHS EARLIER

CASEY WOOD SAT ON AN UGLY GREEN COUCH IN HIS BUDDY'S basement, listening to his friends bicker. Music blared in the background and loud voices prevailed.

"Are you kidding me? It's debates like ours that *created* a movie like *Freddy vs. Jason,*" said Danny Capill.

"Whatever," replied Mark Craver.

"Nah, I'm in the know. Saw an interview. The guy who plays Freddy said so himself."

"Well aren't you just flippin' special," said Mark.

"First *Friday the 13th* movie I ever saw was the fourth," said Cameron Ford. "You know, '*The Final Chapter,*'" he added, fingers raised in the air Mini-Me style. "Five movies before '*The Final Friday.*'" Cameron did the air-quote thing again.

Casey hadn't said anything so far, but now felt the need. "Man, that one was *terrible.*"

"Which?" asked Cameron.

"*Jason Goes to Hell,* the ninth—am I right?" said Jeremiah Bronson. "Wasn't that '*The Final Friday?*'" Jeremiah did *his* impression of Cameron's Mini-Me impression. "Big-time lousy."

"What were they thinking, making Jason's soul jump around from person to person?" asked Danny. "That's not a real *Friday the 13th* movie. Gotta have the real Jason killing people. Dumb move." Danny cracked his knuckles and opened another can of Bud.

Casey, Jeremiah, and Danny all sat on the same ugly green couch, while Mark and Cameron stood. The couch was the lone piece of legitimate furniture in the Fraternal Order of Friday meeting room—a place known in the outside world as the basement belonging to Mark Craver's parents. Casey didn't remember the exact date the Order was established, but this had been their hangout since his freshman year.

Mark spoke up again, "By that standard, one and five aren't real *Friday the 13ᵗʰ* flicks either."

"Five for sure," said Mark. "Some ambulance guy instead of Jason? What was *that*?"

"One's a classic," Casey commented. "How can you say it's not a real *Friday the 13ᵗʰ* flick?" He looked at Mark. "One started it all."

"Who really gives a shit?" asked Neal Jordan. He got up from Mark's yellow beanbag chair and took out his cell, looking a little too Keanu-Reeves-cool.

"I give a shit," Danny responded. He pointed at Neal. "*We* give a shit. That's what we do here. Talk about stuff no one cares about. Got it?" He took a drink of beer and belched.

Neal stared at Danny. "Remember when we used to party with *chicks*?"

"Some of us still do, dude. Not all of us are married like you."

"I have a girlfriend," said Neal. "There's a difference."

"Yeah, you *think*," said Danny.

"Whatever."

"Look, this isn't the Fraternal Order of Babes," said Danny. "It's the Fraternal Order of Friday. We hang out. Talk. Watch a flick. Drink. It's cool, remember?"

Neal shook his head. "I gotta call Trish." He walked out toward the stairs.

"Whipped," muttered Danny, loud enough that only Casey and Jeremiah could hear.

Jeremiah got up from the couch and Eric Vathens sat down in his place. "We going pepperoni tonight?" said Eric. "I'm ready to eat."

Casey, Eric, Mark, and Neal were all juniors at Jasonville High School. Danny, Cameron, and Jeremiah were seniors. Cameron had just rented the eleventh *Friday the 13ᵗʰ* movie, which the Order was going to watch as soon as they could reach agreement on pizza toppings—a task that sometimes consumed half the night.

Mark's mom, LeAnne, worked late on Fridays and his dad was never around. Casey remembered seeing Mr. Craver maybe twice, and he'd known Mark since fifth grade. All told, the Order had free rein in the home, not to mention executive pizza privileges.

At the Order's founding, they'd debated various names: "Fraternal Order of Flick" and "Fraternal Order of Gore" were near-misses, as Casey recalled. But when the seven officially voted the choice was sealed: They would be known to each other as the "Fraternal Order of Friday." Of course, if Danny had mentioned the "Fraternal Order of Babes" back then, who could say what would've happened?

The fact that they all lived in a town called Jasonville was part of the irony of it all, serving as a catalyst for all the Jason-talk.

Danny was the most muscular—and occasionally hostile—member of the Order.

Neal was the one with the hot girlfriend. Naturally, everyone wanted to be him.

Eric was quiet, but always seemed to be watching things.

Cameron acted as the instigator for the Order.

Jeremiah was best at being mediator when Cameron's instigations got out of control.

Mark was Casey's best friend, and the most wily, talkative member.

Casey, of course, considered himself the level-headed voice of reason.

"Do we have a pizza decision?" asked Jeremiah.

"We're not ordering until Don Juan chips in," said Danny, his muscular physique tense.

"Neal already paid," said Casey.

"Well tell him to get off the phone with Cleopatra and get *in* here."

Casey ignored the comment.

"Turn that down, I'm gonna call," Mark yelled. Mark was so scrawny he could almost pass for the original

Jason Voorhees. He pointed at Eric, who was closest to the stereo.

Eric nodded dismissively and turned the volume down a notch.

"Can we start the flick now?" asked Cameron.

"Yes, *please*," said Casey.

"Okay ladies," Cameron said. He stood in front of the TV and held up the movie. "Friday's *Friday*."

"This better be better than the tenth," said Danny.

"Yeah, right," said Eric. He was the lone Order member with a mustache, which made him look a little like a used car salesman. "'Better' like your Homecoming date this year?"

"Least I'm gonna get one," said Danny.

They all laughed.

"I was thinking about asking your mom this year," Eric replied. "I'm sure she won't be busy."

Everyone chuckled again.

"Hey now," said Danny. He threw a fake punch at Eric.

Mark hung up the phone. "Thirty minutes, gentlemen."

"I don't think we qualify for that title," Casey said.

CAMERON STOPPED THE DVD AND FLIPPED BACK TO THE MAIN menu before the credits could roll.

"Wow, that was…dreadful. Utterly," said Danny.

"If you're gonna make a movie called *Freddy vs. Jason*, at least decide who wins," said Jeremiah. "What was the point?"

"For all the hype, I must admit I'm disappointed," said Cameron.

"Some decent kills, though."

"And some of those chicks were hot."

"One bloody slice of Americana," said Casey.

"Still dreadful," said Danny. He opened another beer. "They must be out of ideas. Throw Jason and Freddy together and see what happens? Whatever."

"I kept waiting for the plot to unfold," Mark said.

Several of the guys laughed.

"Right," Danny mumbled.

"Yo, why did Jason have hair in this one?" asked Jeremiah.

"Different actor," said Eric. "They ditched Kane Hodder, dude from the last four."

"But couldn't they at least have shaved the new guy's head?"

"Okay," Cameron motioned for everyone to pay attention, "*Freddy vs. Jason* left a lot to be desired. Big surprise. We've established that—"

"I'm out," said Eric, standing up like he was ready to charge out onto a football field.

"You're not leaving until we do the Fraternal Whopper of the Week."

Eric sat down.

"Now gentlemen, we know that the *Friday* movies have some of the hottest chicks in them, who usually end up dead," said Cameron, "The Whopper question is: If you were going to kill one chick from school, who would it be?"

"Only one?" asked Jeremiah, provoking chuckles.

"Why only one?" asked Mark. "Jason usually kills them all."

"You wanna come up with the Whopper next week, fine," said Cameron, pointing.

"Great question, Cam," said Eric, "Beth Simmons." He nodded. "Definitely."

Neal said, "Not that I'd ever kill anyone, but if I had to pick..."

"You *have* to pick," Cameron said.

"Geena Wolford."

"Dude, isn't she like best friends with your girlfriend?" said Jeremiah.

"Yeah," Neal replied. "So? She totally hates me these days. Always saying stuff behind my back."

"How about Meghan Reed?" asked Mark. "She's the worst tease around. Deserves to die."

"Why?" mumbled Casey, shrugging his shoulders.

"Come on," said Mark, "She won't go out with anyone, except for that college boyfriend she had awhile back. Doesn't put out for anyone. Plus, she's always wearing those tight tops."

"Okay then, any other deserving girls someone would like to select?" asked Cameron.

Jeremiah spoke up, "Claire—"

"Claire Borden," said Eric, beating him to it.

Jeremiah nodded at Eric. "Great minds think alike."

"Yeah, so do you guys," said Danny.

"Don't be stealin' someone else's pick," Cameron said to Eric. "You already chose."

Casey stood up and headed toward the pizza boxes. "Karen Gothman. I hate to say it, but I despise her. I can't think of one good thing she's ever done."

"Seen her mom, though?" asked Mark. "Whoa, babe. I'd like to hang on her chandelier someday."

The group laughed.

"Who hasn't picked?" said Cameron.

"You, for one," said Casey.

"Easy. Ashley Tyler. Next."

"No way, Cam, she's cool," said Casey.

"You don't even know. Just wait awhile. She's not." Cameron scowled, and it appeared the subject was closed. "Who hasn't gone?"

No one spoke up for a moment.

"Just Danny, I think," said Casey.

Everyone looked at Danny.

He took a swig of beer. "Hmm, let's see." He looked around. "I think...Trisha Geller."

Everyone turned to look at Neal.

"Not good," mumbled Mark.

Neal hesitated, then his eyes narrowed and he stared straight at Danny.

"That supposed to be funny?" demanded Neal.

"Not really. It's just my answer."

"Your answer is *my girlfriend*?" Neal stood.

"Don't take it personally, bud," Danny said with a near-perfect mimic of Neal's voice. "It's not you."

For a second it seemed things were just going to blow over, but not this time.

Danny stopped looking at Neal and turned—in a sickeningly casual way—toward Cameron. "Again, as I said, Trisha Geller."

Neal stepped forward.

In a quick burst, Danny threw aside his Bud can, jumped up, and met Neal halfway. They crashed into each other. A pizza box went flying.

"Just 'cause she dumped your sorry a—"

Danny tagged Neal with a right across the jaw, staggering him.

"Son of a bitch!" someone shouted.

Neal came back at Danny with a flurry of punches. The two of them went over the couch, knocking over a lamp and table.

"She...hates...me." Danny spat out each word as he punched. "It's...mutual."

Neal wailed away at Danny's stomach. Danny kneed him back in the chest.

Bodies descended upon the brawl and there was pandemonium. Someone's half-full beer can tumbled through the air. More shoving. Cursing. Whenever the guys would separate Danny and Neal for a second, one of them would rip free and be back at the other.

Neal tried to raise his fist again, but Eric and Jeremiah both grabbed his arm.

Cameron yelled and tackled Danny. "Cool off, dude! Now!"

Danny tried to throw Cameron off, and succeeded partially. But by then, several of the guys had forced Neal over to the far side of the room.

"Guys, we aren't gonna do this!" screamed Jeremiah.

Mark picked up the fallen lamp.

Everyone was breathing hard. Some post-scrap cursing flew around the room. The smell of spilled beer hung in the air like a cheap brewery.

The fight itself had been a draw, but Neal's lip was bleeding and Danny's face was blotched with red marks.

"Real cool!" Neal pointed and shouted from across the room, beer foam in his hair. "Think you're funny saying my girl? Trisha and I are serious, man! I care about her! Don't you ever—"

"She'll rip your heart out and swallow it!"

"You don't know shit!"

"Enough!" screamed Mark. He picked up the tipped table and slammed it down.

Exhales came from all around the room. Eventually, silence.

"You guys riding together?" Casey asked Jeremiah and Neal.

"Yeah," Jeremiah answered, "We're, uh, headin' out now." He pulled Neal's arm. They walked to the stairs and Neal didn't bother to look at Danny.

The room grew quiet again.

Casey scanned around, speechless. He looked at Danny. Soon everyone stared at Danny.

"Nice one, dude," Casey said.

Danny shrugged his shoulders. "It's all just"—he raised his eyebrows—"*pretend* anyway."

A moment later they heard Jeremiah's car start up and tear off.

four

Two days later, on Sunday morning, Casey, Mark, and Neal met up at Casey's house and walked toward City Park, about three blocks away.

"Why do we care about putting in an appearance today?" Mark asked.

"Half the town's going to be there," declared Neal.

"Right." Mark turned to Casey. "Trisha?"

Casey nodded.

"What'd you expect?" said Neal.

The group turned down Meridian Street. Casey watched Mark slip on some earbuds and fire up his iPod, which he believed he could listen to while also walking and gabbing.

Casey asked Neal, "You doing okay after Friday?"

Neal wasn't very good at feigning ignorance. "What happened Friday?"

"I guess...nothing."

"Nothing the Order can't withstand," said Neal, almost to himself.

Casey took in a long breath. He wondered if Neal really believed that or was just saying it.

"Truth be told," Neal said, "I'm more stressed about today."

"Why's that?"

"My parents are meeting her parents...and everyone else."

Casey kicked a rock, soccer-style.

"My thoughts exactly," Mark chimed in, a few decibels louder than necessary. Two steps later he found his own rock and gave it a boot.

"Families getting together," said Casey. "You know what's coming next, don't you?"

Neal stared off into the sky. "Yeah, dude. I know."

They approached the park, where Trisha's family and some relatives were hosting a big shindig. Rumor had it there would be a hot dog eating contest around noon.

Neal glanced at Mark, earbuds still in, then turned to Casey. "Can I ask you a serious question?"

"Hit me, my friend."

"Do you think...I mean...if you were me..." Neal warily studied Mark for a reaction. Mark remained lost in his own distorted guitar world.

"Yeah?"

"Am I too young to get engaged?"

Casey smiled and nodded. "You're asking me?"

"Yes, I am."

"Seriously?"

"Dude, don't take this the wrong way...but I trust your judgment."

"Yo, you're makin' me cry."

"I'm serious."

"Thanks, man. Look, you and Trisha...you guys are good together. I wouldn't worry."

"Hey! Neal's heeeere!" A balding man with a beer belly let out a cheer and rushed over. "Come here, my man! I want you to meet some folks."

"Be right there."

"Right on," the man said with a grin. "How do you do?" He nodded toward Casey and Mark, then turned away and hurried off without waiting for a response.

"One of Trisha's uncles," mumbled Neal.

"Lucky you."

"He like *loves* me for some reason."

Casey chuckled. "And why shouldn't he?"

Neal smiled. "Well, duty calls."

"You da man."

"Hang out awhile," said Neal. "Keep each other company."

"Will do," Casey replied.

"I'll use you guys as an excuse to extract myself after a bit."

"Swell."

"Food should be good. And it's free," Neal said and jogged off.

Mark yanked out an earbud. "Man, is he ditchin' us already?"

An hour later, Mark won the hot dog contest, narrowly out-eating one of Trisha's uncles. Neal finished fourth. Casey opted not to partake, but found all the trash-talking amusing, considering the contents of a hot dog.

The powers-that-be then let all the normal people eat, and the smell of grilled meat teased Casey's nostrils…and stomach. He thought he detected burgers and looked longingly toward the barbecue. He found Trisha sitting alone on a bench, watching Neal play with her twin nieces. Casey sat down beside her.

Mark came over and took a seat on the grass next to them. He groaned.

Casey said to him, "So did you get your grub on today or what?"

"I may puke later."

Trisha laughed. "I think they got those hot dogs from one of the gas stations in town," she offered, "at a special heat-rack discount."

"Now is that any way to talk about your own relatives?" Casey said.

"You can both shut up," said Mark.

"Want another?" asked Trisha, holding up a half-eaten hot dog. "Didn't finish mine."

Mark looked horrified. "I need another hot dog like I need the lint in my navel."

"At least you won," Casey said. "That's the important thing."

"Yeah, just call me the über-dogger." Mark burped, stood, and walked off.

Trisha and Casey chuckled.

Neal was playing keep-away with Trisha's nieces, and doing a great job pretending he couldn't intercept their Frisbee. The park was busy, as Jasonville's version of yuppies mingled about, letting their dogs sniff each other. The town was hopping with one last unofficial post-summer hurrah.

Trisha kept smiling toward Neal. She wore a white blouse and a Hawaiian shell necklace. *Very* petite and *very* nice, Casey couldn't help but notice. And with her yellow sunglasses and blond hair, she looked golden, ethereal. Neal certainly led a charmed life.

Casey spoke, "Ain't your Neal just a stud?"

"He is a sweetie."

Casey watched a squirrel pillage from a pile of discarded peanut shells. A familiar car caught his eye as it drove by the park, but he tried to ignore it.

"Don't take this the wrong way," Casey said, "but I think you've dated more members of the Order than any other girl in school."

"Lucky me."

"If you say so."

"C'mon, what's the record?" Trisha shrugged. "Like two?"

"Could be. I can check."

"Please don't."

"Yep, it's confirmed at two," Casey said. "Hey, you should tell all your friends what a goldmine of men the Order is."

She gazed at him through her golden shades. "Yeah, I'll tell them it's a goldmine with the occasional land mine."

Casey kept quiet. Trisha opened her mouth to say more, but then stopped and sighed instead.

He guessed that Neal had told her about the altercation on Friday. The guys had always had a gentlemen's agreement not to discuss specifics about the Order meetings with those on the outside. Apparently fights and gentlemen's agreements didn't go together too well. He was sure no one else besides Neal would've said anything, and he couldn't really blame Neal for disclosing things to Trisha. As long as it had ended there. Casey watched himself in the reflection of her sunglasses; he did a pretty good job keeping a straight face. He attempted a smile. "Man, I need a burger."

"Then just go get one," Trisha said. "Be sure to load up on onions and burp in Mark's face."

Casey assumed that Neal had also told Trisha what prompted the scuffle. No doubt she had been hurt by it, and now she was trying to bottle it up.

He asked, "So does the goldmine make up for the land mine?"

Trisha watched Neal and the girls before replying, "Well, if you must know, I think at this point in my relationship with Danny, he was taking me out to do shots of tequila, daring me to get down to the worm. Neal and I... it's just way different. We go out and watch the stars and talk."

"Cool. Your gold futures must be bright."

One of the nieces squealed with laughter. Neal lunged at her with alligator arms. Trisha beamed. "Look at him."

Casey pointed. "Do you mean that Neal's good with kids 'cause he plays well with your nieces? Or that he leads a charmed life and is the envy of many?"

"Now, don't start sounding jealous."

"I'm not."

"Good," she said.

"He's my friend," Casey replied. "We're buds for life."

"Great, because while Neal's a wonderful guy," Trisha

said, "you have better things to focus on at this point in your life. Like the people who are jealous of you."

"*Moi?*"

She smiled again, somehow both teasingly and graciously, and right then Casey knew what he'd do if he were Neal. He pictured her in a bright white wedding gown coming down the aisle of a church, himself standing beside Neal, both of them in tuxes, smiling, looking *GQ*-worthy.

"You know what I mean, Casey, really," Trisha replied.

"I do?"

"Yes," Trisha said, "you don't need me putting in a good word for you with the ladies."

"Oh, please."

"C'mon."

"Never hurts to assume there's still work to be done," said Casey.

"Sometimes I think you know way, way more than you let on," Trisha declared. "You're probably the smartest of them all."

Casey didn't know how to respond to that, so he scanned for Mark, who was nowhere to be found. Perhaps off in an alley somewhere, puking.

Then he saw the car again and realized it had been circling the park the whole time.

Danny's red Mustang.

And then he realized something else. Trisha had seen the car the whole time, too. Noticed it without being obvious. He marveled at how the opposite sex could observe something important while maintaining a casual air.

Neal kept playing, blissfully unaware.

Casey met Trisha's gaze and knew they were thinking the same thing. And then he thought he detected something else there. A twinge of fear, maybe?

Danny slowed the Mustang and pulled over to the side of the road, directly across from the park. Cameron was in the back seat, and someone else—Eric maybe—in the passenger seat. He relaxed a little.

Under normal circumstances, if he hadn't been talking with Trisha, he'd probably go over and chat. He spotted Mark heading over to the side of the car to do just that.

Danny was staring his way...almost a menacing stare. Maybe at him. Maybe at Trisha. Maybe at Neal.

Maybe it was Casey's imagination.

The carload of guys and Mark were all talking, nodding, stealing glances. Danny was shaking his head.

Casey turned toward Trisha. He felt some guilt about taking part in Friday's conversation.

Just talk. Idle talk. Nothing more.

His eyes bounced across the group of people in the park. For an instant he thought he saw Karen Gothman's face in the crowd. His eyes widened, then the image was gone. Some girl he didn't recognize stood there instead, sipping a 7-Up.

Mark got into the car with Danny and the guys. Danny smiled their way, then pulled out.

When the car cleared his peripheral vision, Casey said to Trisha, "You know, some people seem to like you both individually, but hate you as a couple."

Trisha stood. "Some people," she looked over her shoulder, toward the spot where the Mustang had been, "need to *get over* it."

five

"WE'RE GOING TO *PUNISH* GRAYSVILLE THIS YEAR!" FOOTBALL captain Kenny Brammer screamed into the microphone, and the crowd roared. The Jasonville High Yellowjacket cheerleaders yelled and bounced in their short skirts. A couple of guys hoisted up the head cheerleader, Meghan Reed, and she performed her windmill arm motions. The remaining cheerleaders led the audience in an impassioned chant.

Every school year they got the chance to mock their rivals in new ways. Tonight it was all about Graysville—this year's opponent in the season opener, and, worst of all, victors over the Yellowjackets for three straight years.

Just south of the high school, in the middle of the practice field across from Stinger Stadium, the crowd surrounded a sculpture in the shape of a "J," for Jasonville. It was a pipe, thickly wrapped with kerosene-soaked gunny sacks. A sweet, flammable scent filled the air.

Kenny Brammer jumped off the makeshift stage, handed a football to a cheerleader, and, with a dramatic flourish, lit the "J" with a butane lighter. The crowd cheered as the flames engulfed a large replica of the Graysville helmet, which was lodged in the middle of the structure.

"Why do we burn our own letter again?" asked Mark Craver.

"Tradition," replied Casey Wood.

"Oh right, I forgot," said Mark. "Whenever people

do something galactically stupid, for no reason at all, it's tradition."

Casey laughed. "Subconsciously, the football team wants to take it in the shorts again," he replied.

"Dude, I'm just here for the chicks," declared Mark.

"Yeah, take a number."

CASEY GREW RESTLESS WITH THE PROCEEDINGS AND GAZED OFF into the crowd. He estimated that half the high school was there. He didn't see Ashley Tyler though, which was a shame.

He had lived in Jasonville since he was five years old, which is to say that all the portraits of his life were painted there. As a boy, he'd been preoccupied with bugs and frogs and salamanders—any slimy amphibian and anything eaten by the slimies. That was before a discovery around age twelve or thirteen: He liked girls even more than the slimy amphibians.

Where's Ashley?

Not that most of the Jasonville babes seemed to notice his discovery, at least until he made it up to legal driving age. He'd thought a lot about what Trisha had told him at the park, in particular his tendency to underestimate himself when it came to girls. Tonight, as he took in the scenery, he had to admit it: High school had been good to him. They say that kids who are good at academics don't get chicks, but it didn't seem to matter in Smalltown, Indiana.

He loved the excitement of girls, the energy, the risk. The hair.

Somewhere in his thoughts about the opposite sex, a voice was trying to get through. And he finally let it prevail.

The whole *seriousness* of the discussion from last Friday night bothered him, something beyond the fact that Danny and Neal had almost provoked a full-scale Order brawl. Some bad blood among friends was surely normal. But…

The girls.

Something wasn't right.

But what was that *something*?

Casey glanced to his left and saw Mark cozying up to some freshman blonde in a leather coat. The dancing flames from the still-burning "J" made her face glow orange.

Well, maybe I'm making too much out of it.

Maybe.

He glanced around again and still didn't see Ashley, a sophomore choirgirl he thought was kinda cute. He'd need to find her later. Ashley seemed to have a thing for him. And he kinda liked it.

The flames were beginning to dim, and the Jasonville High School tradition known as "The Burning of the J" was coming to a close.

"Where's Danny?" asked Mark.

Casey scanned the thinning crowd. "I don't see him."

"You *jerk*!" somebody screamed.

Everyone turned to look.

"Don't touch me!" Meghan Reed shouted, then slapped Eric Vathens. "You unbelievable creep!" she shrieked. She pounded on him some more.

Eric ripped away from her. "Worthless tease!"

Suddenly, Danny emerged, shoving himself between Eric and Meghan. "Cool it, folks."

Beth Simmons came running up and tried to get around Danny to Eric. "I saw that, you pervert!" She threw something at Eric. "I'll kill you, you ever pull anything like that ag—"

"Bring it on, little girl!" screamed Eric.

Casey and Mark stared wide-eyed.

A crowd of people was now watching, but no one knew exactly what had gone down.

"Shut up," Danny said to Eric and pushed him back. "You okay?" he asked Meghan.

She rubbed her thigh and winced. "Get away from me."

"All of you guys, get away," Beth said, pointing. She grabbed Meghan, and they hurried off.

"What was that all about?" said Mark.

"No clue," Casey replied.

The onlookers were beginning to clear out.

Casey and Mark walked over to Danny and Eric. No one was saying much.

Danny ignored everyone but Eric. "What'd you do to get her so steamed?"

Eric didn't reply. Slowly, he held out a small knife.

There was something on the end of the knife, but Casey couldn't tell what it was.

"Oh smooth," Danny responded and shook his head. "Vathens, you're insane." Danny walked away.

Eric lingered for a moment, then headed toward his car.

Casey looked at the knife again. On its tip was a torn piece of cheerleader panties.

Mark groaned.

They both stared at Eric's back as he walked casually away.

"How the hell," Casey said, "did he get that?"

six

It was the first Fraternal Order of Friday meeting since the fight, and all the guys kept stealing glances at Danny and Neal, waiting.

Casey thought they were doing a good job ignoring each other. Maybe too good.

There was no movie that night, one reason being there were no new *Friday* movies to rent. The other was that Mark had schmoozed his cousin at the liquor store, scoring three cases of Bud—a development that created a great deal of excitement. The plan: beaucoup booze, pizza, maybe Leno, and a lot of shooting the breeze.

Another Friday in Jasonville. What a feeling.

The Friday evening football game had been ruled out because of how depressingly bad the team had looked in their opener. The Order sought to rise above the poor pigskin in their own way.

Neal and Cameron got into an animated discussion about the NFL.

"Colts are going back to the Super Bowl this year! No doubt about it." Neal declared.

"Harrison's getting old," said Cameron. "Seems like he's lost a step."

"Don't be dissin' Harrison."

"Colts just need someone like me," Cameron replied. "I run a 4.5 forty, man."

Neal eyed him. "You couldn't run a 4.5 on a moving side-walk!"

Casey noticed that Danny stared when Neal raised his voice. Nothing came of it, but the atmosphere in Mark's basement was tense.

Jeremiah came up to Casey. He nodded toward Danny and Neal, who were standing on opposite sides of the room. "Reminds me of when I was on vacation," he said, "bleeding in the ocean and waiting for dorsal fins to pop up."

"Yeah, I know," Casey replied. "We should keep an eye on them. Pretend Mark would get in trouble if there's another incident."

Jeremiah chuckled. "Yeah, baby." He downed his beer. "Need another?"

"Nah, I'm good."

"Dude, I gotta piss like a racehorse."

Jeremiah hurried off. Casey glanced around for someone to talk to, but everyone was in the midst of other conversations. He took a drink.

Casey certainly didn't think of himself as the coolest member of the Order. Others were more popular at school. But he had plenty of friends, good grades, and a decent relationship with his mom and dad.

He stared at his beer can and pondered how Mark's basement had become such a mainstay in his life.

A couple years back, the youth group Casey had been attending fell apart after its leader got into a nasty spat with some parents. The Order had gradually formed in the months after. Casey's mom and dad didn't know what went on every week in Mark's basement, but what was the harm in that? If he ever had too much to drink, his house was within walking distance. Most everything in Jasonville was within walking distance.

Early in his high school career Casey's parents—actually his dad, but Mom had also agreed—made a deal with him: Keep the "My Child Is an Honor Roll Student" bumper stickers coming, and they'd let the fascination with horror movies slide. He'd kept up his end of the bargain, and so had they.

Casey had seen his first *Friday* movie at Mark's house when he was a sophomore. Mark was also the one who'd turned him on to beer. Casey figured his parents had to know he drank—almost every teenager did—but they never really rode him on it. With some of the Order members' parents, that wasn't the case, and Casey realized he was lucky. He knew it was up to him not to get into trouble with all the booze.

Mark made a loud puking sound. Casey half-smiled and shook his head.

Cameron popped up next to Casey. "Dude, when was the last time we had an Order gathering and didn't watch a slasher flick?"

"Good question," replied Casey. "You're the one with the DVD collection."

"Maybe I should start bringin' some of my porn."

"Dude, my mom would freak if she ever found any of that lying around," said Mark.

Casey replied, "But she's fine with slasher flicks?"

"Not fine," said Mark. "Just unaware."

Neal piped up, "Well, I'd certainly never hear the end of it if Trisha found out we started watching porn."

Cameron stared. "Which she wouldn't because we all follow the Order silence code."

"Some of us don't need to watch stuff like that, anyway," said Danny. "When ya got the real thing." He stared at Neal, then took a long drink of his beer.

"*Not* good," someone said.

Silence.

"Who's he talkin' about?" said Jeremiah, coming back from the bathroom.

"Shut up," said Mark to no one in particular.

Neal didn't take the bait. He spoke to Cameron as if nothing happened, "So, anyway, like I was saying—we should score some tickets and head up to Indy some weekend. You could visit your sister."

Everyone started up again like normal.

Jeremiah eased up to Casey. "Ho, man...can you believe that?" He gestured toward Danny, who was pretending no one should've thought anything of it.

"Maybe we should just find a neutral location and let them go at it, cage-match-style," Casey said.

"Indeed."

Jeremiah plopped down on the couch beside Eric. "Awful quiet tonight, Vathens."

Eric mumbled something to Jeremiah that Casey couldn't quite make out.

Indeed, Eric wasn't saying much. As far as Casey was concerned that was a good thing. He didn't really like Eric much after that stunt at "The Burning of the J."

Nearly everyone disliked Meghan. Appreciated her hotness, yes—liked as a person, no. But still.

Casey took another drink of his beer. He glanced at the TV and felt an odd combination of longing and relief.

Somewhere in the back of his mind, he knew the thing with the horror movies wouldn't last. The Order had run out of new *Friday* movies, and it would certainly be tough to get everyone to agree on what to watch next. But something deeper was bothering him.

It was strange to try to analyze; the attraction to horror flicks. Something in Casey's mind wanted the killer in each movie *not* to win in the end. Somehow even when the psycho got his due, he always did more damage beforehand than Casey wanted. And through all the cringe-worthy scenes, Casey still watched to the final minute...*every single time.*

Was the fascination healthy? Maybe not. At least that's what Casey's parents had told him. But ever since his dad had decided their family wasn't going to "do church" anymore, his parents had stopped riding him on it. And so he watched.

What could it really hurt? It was just entertainment. A brief escape from reality. Letting Hollywood concoct some carnage he could experience for a couple hours, while avoiding the life sentences that would accompany it in the real world. These were the thoughts he had to himself. The ones he'd never voice. The ones that managed to rear their heads again every time he'd planned on forgetting them.

Somewhere he had a moral conscience he knew he'd have to deal with someday. But what was the point now? Not like it was worth rocking the boat with his friends. When college time came, they'd all go their separate ways; Jasonville was like that. Until then, he was just going to enjoy the ride.

Casey often wondered if any of the other guys ever had thoughts like his, ones that remained unspoken.

He looked at Danny, burping and laughing. Danny pretended to spit on Cameron for some reason, who in turn stuck his tongue out.

Probably not.

The basement was starting to stink like spilled beer. Casey was startled by the sound of someone gorging himself on pizza, seemingly right next to his left ear. He turned and saw Mark.

"Dude, could you be any louder slopping that pizza down?"

"What?" Mark replied. He grinned back with tomato sauce in the corner of his mouth.

"Sounds like two eels mating over there," Casey said.

Mark swallowed and patted Casey on the shoulder. "*Man,*" he panned the room and toasted his beer, "have we gotta *do* something."

"Yeah?" asked Casey.

"Really make a splash."

"O...kay."

"Remember when we pulled the Pamida heist?"

"I remember the look on your face when the alarm went off," Casey replied, "and you bolted for the nearest exit so fast the words 'total panic' don't even begin to do it justice."

Mark laughed. "I should've at least grabbed a couple stuffed animals or something. Maybe a Piglet or a Barbie."

"Indeed."

There was a big uproar across the room where Cameron and Danny were talking smack.

"I'm unstoppable on PlayStation *Madden*."

"I would *so* whip you."

Mark leaned in and spoke in Casey's ear. "The Order's gotta pull something like that. Something big."

Casey wasn't so sure, but he didn't want to steal Mark's thunder. "Maybe."

"Dude, listen to you," Mark responded. "You sound like you've forgotten how much fun we had with the Pamida gig."

"Fair enough." Casey smiled. "Part of it *was* fun." He hadn't even graduated high school yet, but was already sounding like his dad's friends, waxing nostalgic. That couldn't be good.

"Dude, we'll come up with a plan later—Hey!" Mark turned. "That's mine!" He rushed over toward Jeremiah, who was holding two beers. They started griping at each other about how many beers an Order member was allowed to possess at a given time.

Cameron walked over to Casey and took in the scene of the various Order members laughing, bickering, and getting more and more hammered. "Maybe we should start another round of gore flicks next week. Maybe the *Halloween* series."

"An idea," Casey replied, "but only the first two are any good."

"True."

"And the third one was trash."

Cameron hesitated a moment. "Aren't we the same group who sat through all of the *Friday* movies?"

Casey smiled. "Point."

"Still, if we went with *Halloween*…" Cameron seemed distracted. "Then I could ask another Fraternal Whopper of the Week about who'd you kill if you were Michael Myers. See what mayhem would break loose down here over that one."

"Let's stick to the movies," Casey said. "Skip the question."

Cameron didn't reply. Without excusing himself, he headed toward the john.

Something about the way Cameron spoke—or maybe the thought he'd expressed, or the overall mood tonight—was telling Casey something. He didn't know precisely what it meant, but he could feel it in his gut.

Casey swallowed some beer hard, gave a post-drink sigh, and scanned the group of guys.

He couldn't put his finger on it, but something had changed.

And the Order would never be quite the same.

seven

"If you're not cheating, you're not trying," declared Rachel Irving.

"Interesting approach to academics," said Meghan Reed.

"Actually I try not to limit my philosophy to school-work."

Some of the stores in downtown Jasonville were having sales. Jasonville's downtown area was a series of ma-and-pa stores in two-story buildings on each side of the town square, which had a park and a small fountain in the middle. It was a nice fall Saturday, and there were clothing racks and other items along the sidewalk this afternoon. The sun was shining, and the slight Indiana breeze could make the skin tingle and feel alive.

"Does that rule also apply to guys?" Claire Borden asked.

"Depends on the definition of cheating," Rachel responded. She seemed thoughtful. "Cheating to *get* a guy or cheating *on* a guy?"

Claire made a *tsk* sound.

The trio walked along Main Street, past Ella's Country Kitchen Restaurant and Shakamak Sporting Goods. They stopped in front of Lacefield Fashion, looking like young goddesses in search of the right price on goddess-wear.

Main Street was Jasonville's oldest, and the only one in town paved in brick, which made a rough, click-clunk sound when cars drove along. Main Street's other claim to fame was more recent: last May, a group of Jasonville High's senior guys had jogged down it one night in their jock straps.

A car honked as it went by, and the girls all turned.

"Who is it?"

"Don't know."

"Who cares? Probably some loser."

They walked farther up the street, past Jasonville Drug and Prime Video.

Rachel had blond hair, wore a shirt that said "Kiss Me Before Your Girlfriend Comes Back," and sported pink shorts. Claire was dark-haired and wore jeans and a blouse, and a wristband that read "Dorks Need Love"—though she probably wasn't the one to offer it. Meghan, in all-white sweats, was the thinnest and could have passed for one of the Hilton sisters. She probably had a future in modeling, if she was smart enough to figure it out.

All three were seniors. All of them were considered "hot" by the majority of Jasonville's male teenage population, for sure.

The person eavesdropping didn't prefer any of them. Still, he followed.

THE UPS MAN ROLLED UP TO A STOP IN FRONT OF CASEY'S house, a white raised-ranch house located on one of the few cul-de-sacs in town.

Before the guy could knock, Casey opened the door.

"Package for Mr. Casey Wood."

"That's me."

"Here you are." He handed the cardboard tube to Casey.

"Thanks." Casey closed the front door and headed up to his room. He unpacked and unrolled his new addition. A minute later he found some tape, and started mounting pieces on the vacant spot next to his window.

A new poster. *Freddy vs. Jason.* Twelve bucks, plus

shipping and handling, courtesy of the internet. Casey had ordered it before seeing the movie...seemed like a good idea at the time. He stood back and admired his room with the new poster.

On his walls were three other movie posters and a *Lord of the Rings* calendar. The month was still stuck on August and needed to be changed.

He had his own television in the corner, which was hooked up to satellite service—the only decent TV option in Jasonville—a cordless phone with caller ID, a computer, and a nice dresser full of clothes. Mark, Neal, and Eric had their own DVD players, but Casey was still working on his parents on that one.

The new poster went well with his red curtains and black bedspread. Casey started to change his calendar.

"What is *that*?" came a voice.

He turned to see his mother in the doorway, with a laundry basket in her hand. She was glaring at the *Freddy vs. Jason* poster.

"Just a new movie poster I got."

She squeezed the basket of whites. "What's it say there at the bottom?"

It wasn't really a question, and Casey hesitated before replying. "Uh, I believe it's 'Winner Kills All,' Mom."

"Oh, please." She rolled her eyes in a way that made him know she wouldn't do anything about his newest acquisition, except maybe complain to his dad. She walked away.

He looked over at the poster again.

Freddy's profile was on the left, his face truly gnarled and disgusting. He brandished his knife-fingers. Jason was on the right, staring back from behind his infamous hockey mask. Jason held up his signature machete and squared off face-to-face with Freddy in a let's-get-ready-to-rumble style. The caption that bothered his mother was at the bottom, below the movie's title.

Casey glanced toward the hall, the way his mother had gone, then back at the poster. He stifled a grin.

Yeah.

Mark would be jealous. Didn't matter the movie itself sucked. And Casey wouldn't disclose where he got it.

On top of his dresser Casey had a framed picture from his Little League days. He went over and picked it up. He scanned the bottom line, which read "Front Row: Mark Craver, Casey Wood, and Neal Jordan."

Casey smiled. He and Mark used to call Neal "Field" Jordan, and everyone on the team assumed the nickname had to do with baseball skills. But that wasn't it...

BEFORE THEY'D EVEN HIT THEIR TEENS, CASEY, MARK, AND NEAL were constantly flirting with trouble. They'd staked out claim to a tree house that had been built across the street from a row of houses, in a tree belt bordering a soccer field. The tree house had been built by a previous homeowner nearby who'd since moved on.

The tree house was hard to get to, and the three of them decided to make it even harder. They devised a way to get into it by climbing up nearby trees and entering through a window. They pulled the rope ladder up into the tree house, cutting off all easy access. The method was ingenious—as Mark had noted when taking credit for the idea—and the tree house became a great place to hang out without being bothered. A precursor to their Order days.

Casey, Mark, and Neal made good use of their hangout almost every day that summer. It was theirs, exclusively—or so they had thought.

Of course, some adult had to come along and ruin it. A balding man wearing a plaid tie and nerdy, old-man glasses from across the street kicked them out one day. And he let it be known, in convincing fashion, that he'd be on the lookout for them if they ever came back.

They tried to argue, but it didn't fly. The man, with great fatherly authority, pointed out all the obvious facts: it wasn't safe, they didn't belong there, young boys like them shouldn't be loitering around, they should get home and help their mothers with chores, blah, blah, blah.

Casey and Mark were content to climb down and slink away. Not Neal.

As the man headed across the street toward his garage, Neal struck a defiant pose in the soccer field and stared.

"What's he doing?" Mark whispered.

"I don't know."

Arms crossed, Neal shouted toward the man, "Can we stand in this *field*!?"

Casey and Mark looked at each other with raised eyebrows and backed away.

The guy seemed flustered, like he didn't know what to do.

Then he erupted. "Who do you think you are, young man? I'm not going to take that kind of crap from you!" He rushed toward Neal.

Neal held his ground, which Casey and Mark couldn't believe.

"Boy, what's your name, anyway?"

"Neal Jordan."

"Well, I know you, Neal Joring! I'm from the school!"

There *was* a kid in Jasonville named Neal Joring, but he was older. Casey kept that to himself and looked at Mark, who was stifling a grin.

The man continued shouting and lecturing, his voice growing nasally, sounding more and more like the teacher in Charlie Brown cartoons.

And Neal just stood firm in the field. Eventually the man walked away.

Casey and Mark erupted in laughter.

Field Jordan. The legend was born.

Casey put the picture down. Some of his best times had been with Neal and Mark. These days Neal didn't seem to be as into the Order stuff as Mark. Ever since he had nabbed his hottie girlfriend, the Order had dropped a notch. It made Casey a little sad, but what could he expect?

He could still count on Mark.

The telephone rang and Casey heard his mom answer it quickly. He wondered if it was his dad, getting the story of the two mass murderers now gracing his son's room. He looked over at the poster.

His parents could live with it. Could be worse, after all. Mark had a *Faces of Death* promo poster on the wall in his room. Casey would play that card, someday, if he had to.

He flipped the calendar ahead to September, and one incredibly ugly orc sneered back.

THE EAVESDROPPER CONTINUED TO WATCH THE GIRLS AND LISTEN in with an amplified listener, a tiny device that allowed him to hear the girltalk from a distance.

A sophomore, Rebecca Lanum, walked past Rachel, Meghan, and Claire. Rebecca's body was…advanced for her age, and she dressed so people would notice.

When she was out of earshot, Rachel said, "Ewww, I don't like that skirt."

"Yeah the pink and black don't work," offered Claire.

The eavesdropper tried not to laugh.

Meghan said, "I'm sooo messed up from last night."

"You?" asked Claire. "C'mon."

The eavesdropper adjusted the volume on his listening device, but Meghan never told the rest of the story. Just chit-chat about clothes.

He kept his distance and kept following, simply because he could.

JUST BEFORE DARK, HE DROVE THE THREE MILES OUT TOWARD Shakamak State Park.

A church display on the outskirts of town proclaimed, "Try Jesus. The Devil will always take you back." He smiled.

He passed the church and rounded a curve about ten miles an hour faster than the posted signs indicated was lawful. *There would be no trying Jesus.*

The trees lining the side of the road began to grow thicker. The full moon fought to get through, but the tree cover won.

He entered the park, and drove around the gravel roads, taking his time, enjoying the breeze that crept in through the driver side window. The signs insisted on fifteen miles per hour—he amused himself by driving half that. There was no hurry. He knew the time would come, and soon. He knew all the shortcuts and routes the park rangers patrolled. He knew all three of the rangers, too. And was certain they'd regard his presence anywhere in the park as nothing but normal. They might halfheartedly want him out and off the premises once full night had fallen, but he had ways around that. There were always ways. And he had the will.

He tapped the brake, then held it down, gazing out. The thick, green forested area was classic *Friday the 13th*. Jason would be proud. He could hide out here and be ten feet from some unlucky victim at any given time. He killed the engine and listened. No, there was no Jason lurking out here in the Indiana darkness. Yet.

He got out of the car. A pair of rabbits nervously chewed weeds a few yards to his right. A mommy bunny and baby. How frickin' cute. His ex-girlfriend would've said *aaawww*.

He smashed his foot down on the gravel road, feigning an aggressive move their way, and they took off.

Worthless hares.

He watched the cute and fuzzy bunnies disappear into the brush.

He certainly wasn't out here looking for anything cute. Cute wasn't on the agenda. Cute got you nowhere. Plus, it was next-to-impossible to maintain.

The moon was now visible in the sky, and he felt at ease, confident.

Dark was good. Life-and-death stakes were even better— high-risk adventure. Tom Sawyer meets Klebold and Harris, except without all the impersonal bullets and bombs, and the wussy suicides. That was his game.

He stopped his car in front of Lake Lenape and got out. He walked to the shoreline and stared out into the water. The night was going to be cold.

He checked around for any people, walked a few feet back and stopped.

In Jasonville lore, running down Main Street in nothing but a jock strap was a cool prank. Soon that was going to be considered minor league.

Yes, this is the place.

He took out his camera phone and snapped a picture.

eight

"Wake up, honey."

Friday morning of the following week, Cameron was in that fog between dream and reality.

"Cameron…Jacob…Ford…"

The words came out in a sing-songy way. Mom, of course. Reality.

Cameron opened his eyes and saw his mother smiling—probably a smile of pity—at him. "I just got a call from the office and need to head up to Indy this afternoon. I thought I might stay and spend the night with Emily and help out. She's almost to the end of her ninth month now and feeling a little overwhelmed."

"Oh, right." Actually Cameron hadn't remembered that his pregnant older sister was due anytime now, but he nodded anyway.

"You're welcome to come up after school and join us."

Gee, that'd be fun. "Thanks, Mom, but I told Mark I'd help him try to fix his CD changer after school today."

She smiled again. "Okay then, see you Saturday, maybe Sunday. I'll call. Emily's number is on the fridge if you need anything."

"Tell her hi for me."

"I will. I need to get going. Don't be late for school." She patted his forehead.

"Right."

Cameron rolled over and rested on his pillow a couple minutes until his mother left.

Then he sprang into action.

He threw on his clothes, and, forgoing the shower, put on his Pacers hat. He snatched a bagel and went out the door.

Cameron thought of his sister, his future nephew or niece, and briefly felt a little guilty. Still, he drove quickly to school.

He saw Mark in the parking lot.

"Change of plans for tonight, buddy."

WHEN THE NIGHTTIME CAME, MARK ANSWERED CAMERON'S door, the stereo blaring with a punk-rock guitar solo in the background. "Yeah!" he shouted over the music and voices. "It's Trisha Geller and Geena Wolford! Yeah, babes! Come in, come in!"

"Is Neal here?" Trisha asked.

"Yes ma'am," Mark said, his speech slurred.

"Where?"

"Uh, in the *house* somewhere. Beer's in the fridge. Make a splash, babes. And drink a lot…especially you." He touched Geena's shoulder as the girls walked away.

Mark turned and saw Cameron looking at him, standing in front of the living room window. Mark grinned back and raised his eyebrows. "Whew! I am stoked, baby!"

Cameron rolled his eyes and took a drink of his Bud.

Mark was closing the door when two underclassmen tried to walk in. "Gentlemen, welcome, party's four bucks each."

CASEY TOOK IN THE SCENE AND WAS IMPRESSED. IT WAS ONE THING to *invite* the entire high school, as Cameron had. It was quite another thing to pull it off.

The very drunk and very underage Sarah Gordon waved at Casey and asked him to guess what color her bra was.

All hail King Cameron.

"*This* schmuck," Sarah pointed toward a group of three guys, "thinks it's pink!"

For a moment Casey wondered what she'd do if he took a guess and was right. He patted her on the shoulder as he walked away. "Be in bed by 9:00, kiddo."

She smiled and giggled. "I might."

Casey considered the validity of his standards—he drew the line at freshmen—rendering the Sarah Gordons of the world off limits. *A shame, really.*

He decided to mingle so he couldn't dwell on it.

Half an hour later, a group of girls that included Rachel Irving, Ashley Tyler, and Brooke Wray were talking in Cameron's kitchen. Being the gentleman that he was, Casey brought them each a Bacardi Silver.

The party was getting wilder. At least one shot glass had been broken at the kitchen table. Some girl had run to the back door to hurl, knocking over a houseplant in the process. More alcohol flowed. Casey was on his fourth or fifth Bud, and despite present company, found himself seriously weighing whether or not to go find Sarah.

Actually, the longer he stood with any one group of people, the worse the urge got. He needed to keep moving.

Ashley was saying something in Rachel's ear, and Casey was waiting to get a word in. The music at the party seemed to be getting louder. He wanted to excuse himself in as charming a way possible.

Some hammered underclassman butted in and asked Rachel if she'd like to get married.

"Maybe if you become rich someday," Rachel said. "And much better-looking."

He stared back, looking stunned.

"Smarter wouldn't hurt either."

He paused, raised his beer cup as if he was proposing a toast, then said, "Whatever you want, baby. I *am rich* right now—got five bucks in my pocket and a quarter in my shoe, in case of emergency." He turned the other direction. "Woohoo!"

Ashley and Brooke both glared at the guy, eyebrows raised.

Casey decided there was no segueing off that and slipped away.

The song "Stacy's Mom" was blaring from Cameron's parents' magnificent Bose speakers. Mark had his own take on the tune, and was screaming in Casey's ear.

"Casey's mom! Has got it goin' on!"

"Shut up, Mark." Casey tried not to laugh.

"She's all I want, and I've waited for soooo long!"

"Jackass."

Geena Wolford walked by, distracting them both with a short top that exposed her still-tanned abdomen.

"Wow, doesn't she just have a great come-blow-yourself-in-me look to her?" said Mark.

Where's Sarah? Casey caught himself wondering. "Yeah," was all he mumbled in response.

Time to move on.

"Yeah baby!" Mark drained his Bud. "Is it just my imagi-nation," he changed gears, "or is this room oozing with envy toward *moi*?"

Mark gyrated and sang some more, not particularly well.

"Your imagination," Casey replied. "Without ques-tion."

Some young guy stood up on a table, beer bottles in both hands, and yelled, "Is there a lonely lady here who needs some attention?"

"Pipe down, asshole," someone replied.

"Get off there!" Cameron yelled.

"What an idiot," said someone else.

Casey laughed and used the moment to ease back toward Ashley and her group of friends.

Ashley was in mid-sentence, "…that's so lame…so Angela Lacy."

"The new girl?" said Geena.

"Yeah, I don't like her," added Brooke.

The girls stopped their conversation to look at Casey. He looked at Ashley and thoughts of Sarah the Freshman flew out of his head. "You look cute in pink, sunshine."

She smiled.

"Who are you?" Geena asked, and Casey couldn't tell if she was being serious.

"Just one of the gals," Casey replied, staying put in their little clique.

"Oh," said Geena, and it seemed that was that.

This was cool. They were too tipsy to care he was listening in.

"What's up with that Angela chick changing schools this early in the year anyway?" asked Rachel. "She's a little… odd."

"You talk to her and she seems like she lives in *four-years-ago* land," Ashley declared.

Someone—Mark probably—turned up the music even louder.

Casey leaned in even closer to Rachel and Ashley, pretending he was really involved in the girltalk. Later he might convert it to pillow talk.

AFTER SEVERAL BEERS, TRISHA GELLER NEEDED TO GO UPSTAIRS to use the bathroom. Neal was over with his buddies carrying on about something guy-related that she didn't care about, and Geena had four guys talking to her, all smiling.

Typical. Trisha went up alone.

The bathroom was at the end of the hall. After she'd

finished, Trisha only got halfway back before someone grabbed her arm and pulled her into a large bedroom. It was dark, but in the moonlight coming through the bedroom window she made out the leering face of Danny.

"Jerk!" Trisha said, trying to wrench her arm free of Danny's grip. "Let go of me."

"What's wrong, babe?"

He reeked of hard liquor.

"I have to go to the bathroom," she said.

"You just went, sweetie."

His grip was too firm; she couldn't pull away.

"Stop, Trisha, just talk to me a minute."

She started to shake her head.

"Look…" He let go of her and took a step back. "Look, listen, I'm sorry if I grabbed you too hard." He sounded almost sad, but she'd seen that sort of thing before.

"Charming, Danny. There's a bunch of drunk girls downstairs. Don't you have anything better to do?"

He ignored the question. "Can't we be friends again?"

"Do you grab all your friends?" she asked. "Or just the really close ones?"

He still ignored her, just like he always had whenever it suited him.

"Please. Can't we at least be friends?"

She sighed. "Friends? *Right*. You never wanted that. You wanted a trophy."

He started to lift his hands up and took a quick step back, almost as if she'd spit at him. "No," he whispered.

"Danny, what do you want? Aren't there enough other girls here for you to make friends with?"

He picked up a Jack Daniels bottle from beside the bed and sat down, looking out the window. "Just walk away then, babe."

Trisha turned to leave.

"I still think about Valentine's Day," he whispered.

"Danny—"

"You were so...nice."

"Stop it."

His face spun away from the window and he glared at her. "How can you be like *that*?"

Because I was just too weak to say 'no,' she thought, but instead said, "I've moved on. You should too."

Danny stood. "Don't tell me what to do."

"I'm leaving now."

"You think Neal doesn't want a trophy?"

Trisha hesitated, then answered, "He loves me."

"Right." Danny laughed loudly. "Love." He buried his face in one hand, kept hold of the Jack with the other. "When we were together on Valentine's, you know you wanted to be with *me*."

"I didn't want what happened."

He threw up his hands. "Then how?"

"I was too weak to tell you to stop."

"Oh..." A haunted expression came across Danny's face. "No way."

"It was the worst mistake of my life."

"No. No way!"

"It's the truth."

"*No!*" Danny threw the bottle against the wall. It smashed and fell to the carpet, and amber-colored remnants of whiskey trickled down from the wall.

Trisha stared at Danny, then back at the broken bottle. Part of it was still held together by the label even though the glass was shattered. She thought of what they once had—or what *he thought* they once had—now broken beyond repair. And the label Danny was still trying to cling to would never have been enough.

They heard footsteps coming down the hall.

Seconds later, Neal and Jeremiah were in the doorway. "I wondered what was taking you so long." Neal flipped the light switch and stopped when he saw Danny. He looked at Trisha. "What's going on?"

For a moment no one said anything.

Danny smiled at Neal, leaned toward Trisha, and spoke in a chiding tone, "Yeah, whatcha doin' with Danny in the bedroom?"

"Shut up!" she said.

"Again," added Danny.

Jeremiah groaned.

Trisha tried to stay calm, but it felt like all the air had just been sucked out of the room.

"What's that supposed to mean?" said Neal.

"Oh, I'm sorry, Neal-y," said Danny. "Didn't you know? Sweet Trisha's never told you about her little indiscretions?"

Neal kept his eyes on Danny. "It's time to leave, Trish."

Trisha didn't know what to say. Inside, she was dying; outside, her eyes were starting to tear up. She felt used.

Jeremiah stared back and forth between the three of them.

Neal stepped forward and said, "Danny, I know you're drunk. We're friends. Or we were once. But let's get something straight. I will *not* hesitate…to rip your throat out."

Trisha quickly looked at Jeremiah, but his eyes were locked on Danny.

Danny stared hazily at Neal for a moment, then said, "Why wait?"

Neal glared back.

No one moved.

Slowly, Neal turned away and headed toward the door. "We're both still young, Danny." He put his arm gently on Trisha, and they walked out.

Someone downstairs had killed the music, and Cameron was clearing people out. The party was over.

nine

TWO WEEKS AND SIX DAYS LATER
TERRE HAUTE, INDIANA
(Thirty-one miles northwest of Jasonville)

TIFFANY MUELLER THOUGHT SHE HEARD A CUSTOMER ENTER THE store. The door had made a sound like it had been opened, but it was very soft. Too soft, in fact, to rattle the bell. She wondered why that would be.

"Hello?"

No one answered.

Tiffany put the racquetball goggles down and walked back toward the checkout counter.

"Hello?" she tried again.

She waited. Had she imagined the door? She scanned the vacant aisles, doubting.

Then, to her left, a squeaking noise.

The old floor at Hoskins' Sporting Goods was wood, first laid in the 1950s. From the sound, Tiffany was almost certain someone had come in. She wasn't sure if that was a good thing.

She spoke loudly, "May I help you find anything?"

No answer. No customer asking her to find jock straps, or sports bras, or basketball pump needles. No one complaining that the pharmacist next door kept bankers' hours.

Tiffany walked slowly toward the rear of the store, stopping near the back room. "George?" she called out, even though she knew the cleanup guy had gone home for the day at least an hour ago.

"Hello? Anyone there?"

She sighed and stood still. Perhaps the customer was deaf, or a senior citizen.

Tiffany made her way back to the front counter, still looking and listening. She looked through the window display. It was getting dark outside.

She turned around. She'd never had reason to notice before, but for a ma-and-pa store, Hoskins' was a fairly big place. Someone could be in here, unnoticed, for a long time if they wanted.

But why would they want to?

She stared down the aisles. She checked the clock. Half an hour before closing time. She glanced around again, then leaned forward and listened. Still nothing.

Sometimes she'd mistaken the sound of people entering neighboring businesses with folks who were actually coming into Hoskins'. She'd had the flu recently and her senses weren't as sharp as normal. Maybe the squeaking had been a mouse. And the furnace made weird sounds sometimes, too. Or maybe a sneaker had fallen off a shelf again.

Tiffany remembered the goggles she'd been stocking and headed back to the racquetball/tennis section. Somewhere between doubt and duty—and her desire to get done and go home—she was able to stay on task.

She stacked containers for a couple minutes, then looked up.

There, across the aisle, she saw him.

She dropped the goggles.

He was looking right at her. He wore a creepy paintball mask, one of the ones they sold in the pellet-gun aisle. But it was the way he stood—tall and menacing, seeming to stare right into her eyes—that chilled her blood.

How long had he been watching her?

She took a half step and stumbled on the goggles. She

looked down to kick them out of the way; when she looked back, he was gone.

Tiffany glanced to the left of where he'd been standing, then to the right.

"Hey! What are you—?"

She thought about yelling something forceful about not hiding out in stores and trying on merchandise, but instead hurried to the counter.

She got to the counter but didn't see him anywhere. Was he a ghost?

No, just some guy in a mask screwing around, right?

Her mind raced. She knew what she was made of and considered herself not easily scared, not one to back down to anyone or anything. Would she let that all fly out the window at the sight of some sneaky guy in a paintball mask?

Tiffany fumbled for the phone while trying to find something under the counter to use as a weapon. Her hand closed on a shrink-wrapped package of cash register tape.

A noise slammed against the counter and jolted her, making her drop the phone. She looked up and gasped.

He was standing at the counter, leaning over it, looking at her. She hadn't heard any footsteps.

He no longer wore the mask. A young, dark face, clean-shaven, with a narrow jaw and intense eyebrows, stared back. The mask was on the counter, the guy's hand on top of it, palming it almost like a basketball. Next to it was the box he'd gotten the mask from.

Tiffany rose, trying to position herself face-to-face, clerk-to-customer. After all, it wasn't that uncommon for some guy from ISU or elsewhere to drop by the store and pick up something for silly college boy adventures.

"All ready, " he said.

She tried to compose herself, but his voice—cold and raspy—seemed to reach in and snuff out her breath.

Tiffany took the item to ring it up and that's when their eyes met.

Black.

The blackest eyes she'd ever seen.

Unreal.

They were not human. The temperature in the room seemed to drop thirty degrees, but her face felt hot.

Her fingers managed to scan the item and ring up the total. She remembered something from when she was in nursing school—before she'd dropped out—about how some kinds of drugs can make a person's pupils dilate, others shrink. What were the ones that can make eyes black? Heroin? Coke?

She quoted him his total and studied him as he paid. There was no way this guy was on something. He was steely cool.

He reached into the front pocket of his worn, black jeans and pulled out cash. He handed it to her, and she made the mistake of looking into those animal eyes again. He almost smiled…or sneered.

The lights in Hoskins' Sporting Goods seemed to flicker. Tiffany's lungs felt tight.

She started to give him his change.

"Thanks for coming in," she lied.

"Thank you," he whispered.

The cold, raspy voice unnerved Tiffany, and she accidentally dropped the coins on the counter. "Sorry."

She frantically picked them up and put them in his gloved hand without looking at his face. His other hand was caressing the mask—a little too fondly.

"I think that's it," she said, then exhaled.

The guy didn't seem to care about his receipt, or a bag, and she wasn't going to ask. He slipped quickly out the door.

Tiffany took a step back.

She had the distinct feeling that something unholy had come into Hoskins' Sporting Goods today. And she didn't like it for one second.

ten

FRIDAY, OCTOBER 12
9:02 P.M.

"They're making a twelfth *Friday* sequel?" asked Jeremiah, incredulous.

"Maybe not technically," Casey said. "It might not be another *Friday the 13th* sequel in the chronological sense."

"Kinda like *Freddy vs. Jason*?" interrupted Mark.

"Rrright," said Casey, doing his best Dr. Evil impression.

"Can't wait," Mark droned without looking away from the TV.

The scene in Mark's basement was more subdued than usual. Several of the guys either weren't there yet or weren't going to come this week.

"Just like the last one, it probably won't make it to our prissy little theater," said Casey. "But I was reading this stuff on the web about it. Rumor has it Freddy's out to get revenge for, you know, Jason cutting off his head and all."

No one said anything for a moment. "Jason didn't cut off his head, though," declared Jeremiah.

"Huh?" Casey said.

"I thought they were going to try a prequel or remake or something, not another Freddy-Jason thing," Mark interjected.

"As I was saying, it was that blond high school babe who beheaded Freddy," said Jeremiah.

"Oh yeah, you're right," mumbled Casey.

"Hey, wasn't *Freddy's Revenge* the name of one of the *Nightmare* sequels?" asked Jeremiah.

"Only good *Elm Street* movies were the first and third," Mark declared. "The rest sucked." He stared back at the TV. "*Freddy vs. Jason 2*...wonder who wins this time? Just can't wait."

"They could call it *Freddy vs. Jason 2: The Final Cash-In*," Jeremiah added.

Casey smiled. "Another *Friday* film will probably come out before we graduate," he said. "Another great slice of Americana."

"Pfft." Mark looked over at them and shook his head.

Jeremiah chuckled. "What the hell is 'Americana' anyway?"

Casey shrugged.

"Bad horror movies, man," said Mark.

Jeremiah glanced around. "Where *is* everybody?"

"Dunno," replied Casey. He looked at his watch. "But if no one else shows up, I'm bailing for Ashley's."

"Oh?" inquired Jeremiah.

Casey smiled. "Said she'd be home later."

"Yeah, well we'll want the details," said Jeremiah. "Actually we need to have a full Order debriefing. And not just from you."

"Right, maybe that'll get everyone here again," Casey said.

Jeremiah spoke, "Ever since that new babe started working at Cassandra's Pizza, Danny's been blowing us off."

"Nice for him to leave more pizza and beer for us though," commented Casey.

"Pah," replied Jeremiah.

"Yeah, but I'm kinda sick of it..." Mark trailed off and looked around. "Something's gotta change, though...*something...anything.*"

11:39 P.M.

BETH SIMMONS THOUGHT SHE HEARD A NOISE AS SHE GOT HOME from work, but couldn't be sure.

The house was totally dark. Mom must be getting in very late tonight.

She walked through the front door and felt a breeze.

Coming from *inside* the house.

"Hello?" she called out.

She walked into the kitchen and flipped on the light.

The back door was open. The doorknob was mangled, and there was splintered wood everywhere.

She gasped. A burglary? In Jasonville? Or something worse? She ran the other direction.

Get out now, get across the street to the MacKensie's.

She made it back to the front door, but before she could go through it, she saw a shadow out of the corner of her eye. It came at her so fast—she had no time to respond.

Beth felt a searing pain in the back of her head.

Then blackness.

HE CLOSED THE FRONT DOOR, BUT DIDN'T BOTHER LOCKING IT. HE stared down at the floor.

The very gorgeous and very popular Beth Simmons lay motionless.

It was all so quick. Almost like it hadn't really been him.

He crouched and gripped the handle of the hammer.

Just like one of Jason's.

Unlike Jason, he couldn't risk leaving it behind.

11:48 P.M.

GEENA WOLFORD WAS ASLEEP ON THE COUCH IN FRONT OF THE TV.

All was otherwise quiet in the Wolford home. Sweet Geena's parents were snoozing away.

He slipped in through the garage. No one, it seemed, bothered to lock their doors in Jasonville.

No one.

He crept to the couch.

He raised his spear.

A moment later he turned off the television and left.

11:59 P.M.

It was beginning to rain.

Claire Borden couldn't find her Pink CD, so she headed outside to look in the car.

She rummaged around. Where had she left it?

Claire heard someone behind her, but figured it was someone just walking by. The sound ceased.

She realized the light scraping of footsteps on the pavement had stopped right by the car, and that made her feel uncomfortable.

Claire gripped her keys in her hand. She was going to be ready, just in case. She flicked off the safety latch on her pepper spray keychain.

As she turned, she felt a sense of dread.

There was a man in a hideous mask, standing right in front of her. She raised her hand and sprayed, screaming, aiming for his eyes.

Goggles.

The ax came down way too quickly.

eleven

HE WATCHED MEGHAN REED THROUGH HER WINDOW. SHE SAT on her couch talking on the phone, wearing her "Britney Bites" shirt.

A car pulled in at the neighbor's house, and the headlights annoyed him. He slipped away from the window and into the bushes at the side of the house.

Eventually, quiet returned. He knew her parents were probably home, and that he'd have to be patient. But the right moment would come.

A noise startled him.

Someone was coming out of the house.

He saw long blond hair and a yellow and black coat. As in the Jasonville High *Yellowjackets.*

Meghan was headed down the sidewalk.

This was going to be easy. He followed her.

The sidewalk and street were dark. The rain washed out the night sounds and helped him sneak up close.

He crept forward and caught up with her, so close he could hear her breaths.

Meghan was directly in front of him.

"Bitch," he said.

Startled, she turned around.

He'd already cocked his hand back with the cleaver, and brought it down forcefully.

Just as he realized that the girl was *not* Meghan Reed.

12:22 A.M.

AFTER NEAL LEFT HER HOUSE, TRISHA GELLER SETTLED INTO BED with a book. Her parents were out of town and she wished he could have stayed. But his parents wanted him home by 12:30.

Five minutes into her book, she heard a loud crash. It seemed to come from the garage.

"Neal?" she said. Her unease grew as she walked downstairs.

She stepped into the living room. The only sound was the hum of the refrigerator.

Trisha walked forward. "Sweetie, is that you?" she called as she opened the door that connected the house to the garage.

She flipped the light switch expecting to see a cat or something. Maybe a raccoon. Or worse, a rat.

The light didn't work.

She flicked the switch up and down several times, as if that might help.

"Neal?" she tried again, though she knew he'd driven off five minutes ago.

She looked around the dark garage, then toward the ceiling. From the glow of nearby streetlights, she could see that the garage's light fixture had been smashed. Her mouth dropped.

She stepped to her dad's tool table and grabbed a flashlight. She shined it around and saw nothing.

Trisha stared out of the garage and down the driveway.

Animals don't shatter garage lights.

She stepped back to the doorway and pressed the button to close the main garage door.

Trisha watched the door lower slowly and wished it would hurry. She half expected some juvenile delinquent to burst in before it closed and give her the finger.

Then she thought she heard another sound. A scraping noise that was out of place.

She tried to sense where it had come from. It was hard to pinpoint with the commotion from the garage door. To her left, through the house maybe. Coming from the backyard… or the back door.

She stepped back in the house and started to close the door to the garage, but hesitated. The house seemed a little too dark.

Trisha flipped on a light and peered around the corner toward the back door.

It was open. Standing inside the house was a tall shadow of a person. She screamed.

The shadow began to run toward her.

"Get away from me! Oh, God!"

Trisha knew he would beat her to the front door if she tried it, and the garage was a dead end. She ran toward the stairs. Halfway up, something slashed at her legs and she felt a stinging pain.

"No! Please, no!"

She reached the upstairs hall, ripped a picture frame off the wall, and threw it at her attacker.

Then she saw the terrifying, droid-like mask, and the machete.

She screamed again and threw another picture as hard as she could at his head. He stumbled.

Trisha ran into the bathroom, slammed the door and locked it. She sat down and braced her legs against the door, the sudden flexing and pressure of her muscles causing her slash wound to explode with pain. She grabbed a washcloth off the counter and held it against her bleeding calf. She held firm and tried to think.

A moment passed.

Would he go away?

She held her breath.

A shadow appeared in the crack at the bottom of the door. She let out a whimper. The doorknob shook.

Trisha looked at the window. It was one of those huge windows that opened by holding in two spring-loaded latches and sliding the glass up. It was hard to do when someone *wasn't* chasing you. And the jump down would be pretty far.

The bathroom door shook. She didn't think it would hold long enough for her to make it out the window.

"What do you *want* from me?"

She kept her foot against the door and frantically yanked out the sink drawers until she found what she was looking for: a pair of long-bladed scissors.

She grabbed them in her fist and held them up like a knife. Compared to what he had it was pitiful, but if he tried to chop through the door, she was going to stab like crazy the second he reached his hand through.

Trisha spotted her curling iron and plugged it in to the nearest outlet.

There was a loud banging against the door. She gripped the scissors even tighter.

Where was her cell phone?

In my purse downstairs, that's where.

But *he* didn't know that.

"Hey asshole, I have a cell phone in here and I just dialed 911! You might wanna get outta here, now!"

He pounded on the door harder.

Mistake.

"Go away, now!" she screamed.

She touched the curling iron. Not hot enough.

She stared, terrified, at the door and clenched her teeth.

The pounding slowed. Like he had tried to slice through, but the door wouldn't give. A minute later it stopped completely. She stared at the door and felt a twinge of relief.

Then there was some strange twisting sound, something rustling against the doorknob, then nothing else.

She looked at the doorknob. It was still firmly locked.

Trisha held her breath. She couldn't see the shadow under the door anymore.

Silence.

Had he given up on getting in? Fled out of fear of the police?

Or was he waiting just a step away from the door?

More silence. It was too quiet. Trisha gazed at her bleeding leg and let out a cry.

She sensed his presence. He was still somewhere in her home, even though she could see and hear nothing.

She waited.

Several minutes passed.

Nothing.

Her leg throbbed and she was beginning to feel light-headed. She knew she had to get out of the house.

Slowly, she moved her foot away from the door.

Still nothing.

The television in her parents' room across the hall came on. The volume was cranked to the max.

What was that?

It was Geraldo. She could hear it well, on at full blast. Geraldo Rivera on Fox News.

What's he up to?

She barely heard it—the sound of a door opening downstairs, like someone had gone out of the house.

Had the guy in the droid mask left?

The TV blared.

Why would he turn on the TV and leave?

Trisha sat bleeding in her bathroom, trying to focus her thoughts on several possibilities.

She didn't like any of them.

Velma Moorer awoke to the sound of a scream. She sat up and listened, making sure it wasn't a dream.

She heard a second shriek, off in the distance. Definitely not an animal. Definitely human. Something was wrong in Jasonville tonight.

Velma got up to check on Tommie. Hopefully he'd slept through the noise. Tommie, her true baby, with his frizzy, little-boy hair and cute brown eyes. He still slept with the same black teddy bear his Nana had given him for Christmas when he was three. He was all she had left since her husband bailed and that wicked social worker had convinced the cops to take her firstborn away. She came to his room and peeked in.

She stepped forward. "Tommie, honey, you awake?"

Tommie was not in his bed.

TRISHA WAS STILL AFRAID TO OPEN THE DOOR.

She was hating the noise, too. Nothing against news programs or anything.

She looked at her bleeding leg, and the mess she'd made on the white tile floor. The washcloth was soaked. She realized her breathing was getting more labored.

She eased over to the window, eyeing the door nervously.

Trisha set the scissors down on the counter and unlocked the window. She slid the guides in and heaved up. She turned back and gazed at the door.

Nothing.

She went to dislodge the screen. It fell, hitting something on the way to the ground.

Suddenly, sickeningly, everything made sense.

The guy with the mask and the sword had used her father's stepladder to climb to her window. He was only a few feet below.

The TV…the noise.

She shrieked.

To distract her.

Trisha tried to push the ladder off, but he leaned up against the house. Too heavy to move.

"Help me!" she cried out into the night.

She tried to close the window, but he blocked it with the machete, then jabbed at her thigh. Trisha lurched back.

She screamed and ran to the door. She unlocked it, but it *wouldn't open.*

She pulled and jerked and pulled some more.

He was almost to the top.

"No!"

Trisha braced her feet against the wall and pulled on the knob with both her hands. She screamed, pulled, and shoved off with her feet.

The door gave a half inch.

She saw an electrical cord was wrapped around the knob.

The twisting sound…the rustling.

"No way!"

A gold lamp cord from her parents' room, wrapped around the knob. And God-knows what else. Trapping her.

How could she be so—?

Trisha turned to the window. He was nearly in.

She remembered the scissors and snatched them off the counter. He jabbed the machete at her again. *The blade was so damn long.* She might never get close enough with the scissors. She threw a shampoo bottle at him instead.

Trisha rushed back to the door, shoved the scissors through the opening, and began cutting.

The cord was tough.

She kept cutting.

She looked at the window again and was sure he was smiling behind his mask.

The wire was fraying.

He was halfway through the window.

Trisha pulled as hard as she could. The cord gave.

She heard him land on the floor.

Trisha flew out the door, just as he lunged for her.

She ran down the stairs and to the front door.

Which he'd blocked with their sofa.

She ran to the back door.

Blocked.

She heard him coming down the stairs and screamed. She ran toward the garage.

Freedom.

She rushed in and hit the garage door switch. She stumbled on the steps and fell hard.

Her ankle. Her legs. The pain. She struggled to get to her feet. The garage door was rising and she began crawling toward the opening.

Then the door started to come down.

"No!"

She looked back in terror and saw him standing in the doorway. He'd obviously been in here before and knew exactly where to find the button.

He pounced at her and swung the blade, cutting her forearm and narrowly missing her face.

Trisha kneed him in the groin.

He groaned and fell. She ignored the pain, the dizziness, and pulled herself up. She shouted, "Help!" as the door closed. The driveway disappeared from view, the only light now coming from the house.

He got up.

She looked around in desperation. A table. Some oil. An empty beer can. She knew all the good stuff was on the other side of the garage.

He stepped closer and raised the machete.

She looked again. Same table...same oil...same beer can.

She fell backward against the table and felt something. She looked down, dumbfounded. A saw.

She swung. He swung.

She grazed him just enough in the side of his neck to throw him off.

The saw came out of her hands on the follow-through.

He staggered but didn't drop the machete.

She took advantage of his stagger and limped back into the house, slamming the door behind her and locking it.

Trisha hurried to the phone. She was about to dial and

then heard the sound of the main garage door opening.

She brought the cordless with her and dialed 911 as she peeked out the front window.

He was running away, holding his neck.

Trisha exhaled and she burst into tears.

The TV was still blaring.

Before anyone came on the line, there was a pounding knock on the front door, startling her so badly she dropped the phone.

"Is anyone there?" the female voice on the phone asked.

"Trisha?" came the voice from the other side of the door.

Someone had finally heard her screams.

"Hello?" said the voice on the phone.

"Trisha! It's me! Are you okay?" came the voice from outside.

She recognized the voice and felt relief.

"Yeah, I'm coming," she called back.

She pushed the couch out of the way.

"What's going on, Trisha? I heard screaming. Wanted to make sure you're all right."

She opened the door.

"I—"

Her mouth fell open.

No!

All she saw was a mask and the streaking reflection of a machete blade, coming toward her neck.

VELMA SEARCHED EVERY ROOM IN THE HOUSE AND TOMMIE WAS nowhere, not even downstairs playing video games. She went back to his room, growing more frantic every second. She hoped he'd magically be back in his bed, but no. Her eyes darted around the room.

She noticed that the bedding had been dragged in the direction of the window.

The window was open a crack. Her mouth fell open. Tommie's window was missing its screen.

She hurried over to have a look out, and a chill hit her. Fear came in and hissed in her ear. Velma stared into the night.

She inhaled something bad, cold.

The screaming she'd awoken to seemed even more frightening. She rushed down the hall toward the telephone.

12:38 A.M.

HE WATCHED CASEY WOOD AND ASHLEY TYLER CAREFULLY.

It didn't look like Ashley would be alone for a while.

He heard a car in the distance and decided to wait at the stoplight.

If nothing came of it, he'd head back.

12:46 A.M.

HOPE REDMOND DROVE DOWN TENTH STREET AND STOPPED at the intersection. She waited for the light to turn, even though there was no traffic.

Hope saw the cross-street light turn yellow and thought about how good it would feel to get home and get her contacts out of her eyes. They felt like Saran Wrap.

A shadow appeared beside her and suddenly her car door was open. She turned and let out a yelp.

Someone in an ugly mask was reaching in, trying to get at her. She saw a flash of metal. A knife?

He stabbed her shoulder. She screamed.

Hope tried to punch her foot down on the accelerator but had to dodge the knife that was coming toward her neck. He was halfway in the car, which floated forward and to the right. He jerked the emergency brake. She tried to scramble out the passenger side, but he stabbed her in the rear. The pain from the blade exploded, unbelievably hot and wrenching. She screamed as loud as she could. He stabbed again, but she blocked the knife with her foot.

Her geometry book was on the floor of the car. She grabbed it and threw it at him. The hardcover book, all 1,000-plus pages of it, collided with his head and snapped it back.

He let out a groan.

The blow turned his mask to the side, and he stopped his attack to straighten it. She shoved open the passenger door and ran.

She looked back.

He jumped up.

She screamed.

She couldn't run very well. He was going to be able to run just fine.

"No!"

She looked around. She was close to a park. Lots of trees, bushes.

She looked back. He was coming her way.

Hope cleared a corner, losing sight of him. She knew that it wouldn't last long.

She saw more bushes.

It was either this or another thirty yards of running until the knife caught up.

As quickly as she could, Hope backtracked a little and hid.

HOPE LISTENED FOR THE SOUND OF FOOTSTEPS AS LONG AS SHE could stand to. She felt that nowhere in the park was safe. She tried to lie completely still and not breathe.

Someone's porch light came on across the street. A man walked across his lawn with a rake in his hand and stopped at the curb.

Her attacker had run off. He'd run into the shadows,

into the shadows where she couldn't see. Still, she sensed his presence nearby.

She'd wanted to scream. Nothing had come out.

The man with the rake yelled something in the direction of his house, then went inside.

She wanted to make a break for the house, but it was far enough away that she was too terrified to try. *He* might pick her off if she made the wrong move.

She stared into the shadows, leery.

Where was he?

CASEY WALKED UP THE SIDEWALK THROUGH THE JASONVILLE night, feeling an odd mixture of guilt and physical relief. He certainly liked Ashley, yet somehow he felt differently toward her now. He did not understand why.

The guys would think he was cool when he told them what had happened. Deep down he didn't feel that cool.

He stepped over a puddle on the sidewalk and was glad the rain had stopped in time for him to walk home.

No real man ever felt guilty about getting into a girl's pants, did he?

Casey didn't have long to dwell on Ashley. He saw another girl running toward one of the houses on the block. He did a double take and realized it was one of his classmates, Hope Redmond. At first he thought she might be drunk, staggering and casting frequent glances behind herself.

That's weird.

He wondered if she was so out of it that she was about to stumble into the wrong house. That almost happened to Mark once. Hey, it was a Friday night, after all.

Actually, Casey realized, it was Saturday morning.

She was nearly to the front porch. He hurried to catch up with her.

twelve

DEPUTY LORRAINE BARRETT HELD UP THE NEWSPAPER, brandishing it like she was bringing down the Ten Commandments from Mount Sinai.

"Chief, I can't believe this. Till now the weirdest thing in the years I've been here was prob'ly that UFO sighting in the summer of 2000. Now this? In Jasonville friggin' Indiana, all of 2,500 people. My mother thinks I work somewhere safe. Now we're—*you're*—featured on the cover of every other paper in the state, not to mention the homepage of usatoday.com."

Bertrand Rix winced from behind his desk. The two of them were in his modest corner office at the Jasonville police station. It was mid-morning on Saturday, approximately nine hours after he'd almost died in Tyre's Tomb.

Deputy Barrett dropped the paper onto the desk. "The Jason of Jasonville," proclaimed the headline of the *Terre Haute Star*.

"How's the girl?" Rix asked.

There was a pause. "Still in the hospital," she replied, almost in a whisper.

Rix gazed out the window. "I hope she pulls through." He shifted in his chair. "She got it worse than I did."

"Speaking of which, boss, you know you don't have to be here today. I can cover for you. Anything, you name it."

"Lorraine—"

"What did Doc Brooks say about your shoulder?"

"Look—"

"Probably that you needed *rest*."

Rix spoke firmly, "I need to be here today for a lot of reasons." He took a long sip of coffee. He set the cup down and stretched his shoulder a little. "It does ache like crazy," Rix admitted.

"Could've been even worse, Chief, for you and the girl," said Lorraine, and they both knew what she meant.

Rix sighed. "I got two agents from the Indiana Bureau of Investigation coming in for a meeting later. All those media people on the front lawn are making us look like the Simpson case. And the Greene County Prosecutor's office has already left me four messages."

"I know," said Lorraine. "Hayes and Wilkins should be back in an hour, by the way."

Rix nodded. "Never been stabbed, have you Deputy?"

She looked surprised. "No."

"Think about that one a minute. Then think about Beth Simmons, Geena Wolford, Claire Borden, Karen Gothman, Trisha Geller, and Hope Redmond. That's why I have to be here."

Lorraine didn't reply.

Rix stood up and tossed his coffee cup in the trash with his good hand. "Sorry if I seem a bit pissy this morning." He patted her shoulder. "Didn't get much sleep last night." Rix made his way toward the door.

"Chief?"

"Yeah?"

"I know I speak for all of us when I say I wish we could've got there sooner," Lorraine said. "You did a gutsy thing."

"Don't worry. Nothing more you could do."

"We've got him because of you," said Lorraine, nodding in the direction of the station's holding cells. "Behind bars."

"Indeed." Rix frowned, started to leave, then stopped.

"We have a name yet on that kid who told Mrs. Marchete to call an ambulance for Hope Redmond, then ran off down the street?"

"Not that I know of. I'll talk to Hayes again."

"Find out who he is."

"Yes, Chief."

"Then pay him a visit and find out what else he knows."

Rɪx ᴛʜᴏᴜɢʜᴛ ᴛʜᴀᴛ ᴀ ʙʀɪᴇғ ᴡᴀʟᴋ ᴍɪɢʜᴛ ʜᴇʟᴘ ʜɪᴍ. Hᴇ ᴅɪᴅɴ'ᴛ want to deal with anyone from the media right now. He remained indoors and his thoughts kept him troubled.

He poured himself another cup of coffee, then headed down the hall, toward the holding cells.

Rix knew he could've easily died last night. He couldn't help wondering why he hadn't been stabbed in the back of the neck, or somewhere more deadly. Why had he been so lucky when others had lost their lives?

He thought about the sobbing parents, the cries, the pain. Rix thought about the shocked community, his overwhelmed staff, his wounded shoulder, his wife's worried face. Nothing seemed real, just the smell and taste of his coffee and the echo of his footsteps down the hall.

The Jasonville Police Station had four small holding cells, vacant more often than not. Rix stopped in front of the lone occupied cell.

The kid, the murderer, the "Jason of Jasonville," was asleep.

Rix still couldn't believe it.

He blinked and thought he saw a vision of a neighbor boy one autumn years ago, catching a football, prancing around in the leaves, and laughing with his friends.

Rix took another drink of his coffee. He stared down at the idle face of Cameron Ford and swallowed hard.

thirteen

KEVIN GIBSON DROVE DOWN INDIANA STATE HIGHWAY 59 ON
Sunday morning, ticked that his buddy Carlson would be
doing a story live from Colts headquarters in Indy today,
while he had to follow this piddly, insignificant little route
to nowhere: Jasonville, Indiana.

Kevin was thirty-one, fancied himself good looking, but
in honest moments realized he'd downed a few too many
meatball subs. He was still trying to get his new Hyundai
Tiburon to adjust from interstate speed to highway, but the
Tiburon seemed to be winning. Kevin wasn't too worried.
The Indiana State Patrol was nowhere to be seen.

The radio was set to an AM talk program, *The Laura
Ingraham Show*. She could usually set him off, but he found
himself oddly attracted to her. Something about the idea of
an off-limits, *verboten* conservative diva held appeal.

This morning very few cars were competing with Kevin,
and he found himself tuning out Laura and gawking out
the window.

The trees and crop fields along the road were showing
the wear and tear of fall. Branches had few leaves left. A lot
of crops had already been harvested, everything but the
corn. Some of the fields had huge bales of wheat straw scattered throughout. Crows hung out by the side of the road,
oblivious as he drove past. The scenery was classic, rural
Indiana—not very vibrant or exciting. Kevin was used to
billboards and skyscrapers.

He glanced at his cell phone, which was mounted on

the car's graphite gray dash, and thought about calling his buddy. Maybe Carlson had forgotten to set his phone to vibrate again, and his ringer would interrupt some important press conference. Everyone would look at him like the clown he was. Kevin could only hope.

Somewhere over the past five miles his phone had gone from three signal bars to "Analog Roam" to "No Service." *Stinkin' Verizon.* Kevin made a mental note to bird the TV the next time the "Can you hear me now?" guy came on.

He couldn't help wishing he was Carlson. What reporter in his right mind wouldn't rather be schmoozing with NFL players like Manning and Harrison this time of year than traveling to the middle of nowhere for a story others were already covering?

You, Kevin, you jackass.

Indeed, he knew the question wasn't whether or not he'd be the first on the scene, or the first to write some puff piece on the Jasonville tragedy. Was there anything more to uncover? He might have to shake off some rust if he was truly going to find out.

Just when he'd thought he'd had enough of being an unknown sportswriter, his career had taken off. The dizzying cycle had begun a year ago when he told his boss he wanted to take a crack at the investigative end, just in time for a sexual assault and booze scandal at Butler University.

In some corners of the world, Kevin was a minor media celebrity. He had doubts about the level of notoriety that awaited him in Jasonville.

Keeping a low profile during investigative work was important, if for no other reason than it helped to keep the death threats away. Kevin's biggest splash and greatest curse came when he broke the sex scandal at Butler University involving basketball players and recruits. The story got picked up statewide first, then nationally. Kevin was featured on TV and radio so much that even he got sick of seeing himself. Meanwhile, Butler officials were issuing denials, but still canning coaches and dismissing players. When March Madness came and the depleted Butler team got their asses handed to them early in the tournament, the backlash began. Kevin and the Indy *Tribune* were no longer crusaders for truth in the public's eyes. No, suddenly they were marauding forces of smear and destruction, seeking to attack a fine educational institution—and worse yet—in favor of bad basketball.

So concluded the life of Kevin Gibson as an investigator of local sports scandals. The joke around the office was "Anything but the truth" when it concerned a nationally recognized basketball program. Andrew O'Malley, Kevin's boss, had straddled the line between faith in his reporter and good P.R., and Kevin got reassigned to "true crime" investigative stories. It was great—when there was something worth investigating. Lately he'd covered a series of duds. Meanwhile, his friend and former underling, Shade Carlson, now got all the plum sports assignments. *Lucky schmuck.*

Hopefully no one in Jasonville would give a rip that Kevin had gotten Butler's star guard kicked off the team last spring. Hopefully, no one in Jasonville would know *anything* about him.

THE RADIO BEGAN TO CRACKLE, AND LAURA'S NASALLY "I LOVE you, Kevin" voice was fading.

Now what? He considered switching the stereo over to CD, but instead reached for his phone. Still no service.

Perfect. Just perfect.

No cell phones. No radio. No signs of human life.

Kevin looked at the road and sighed. Hadn't he passed a sign about fifteen minutes ago saying Jasonville was only four more miles?

To his left, something big caught his eye.

A huge, intimidating cornfield lined the view to the east. It stretched out across what seemed to be half of Indiana, with cornstalks that were easily over eight feet high. But it was what appeared above the field that really grabbed Kevin. Thick, billowy fog hung in the air, like some strange cloaking force. An ominous, opaque painting.

Kevin killed the stereo. The highway seemed to get narrower. Kevin slowed the car. He knew he should watch the road, but he couldn't help staring.

A car whizzed by his Tiburon and honked.

Too close.

Kevin realized his hands had tightened on the steering wheel, and that he was going well under the speed limit. He looked back toward the shrouded corn one final time.

What awaited him in Jasonville?

He accelerated and tried to find anything other than static on the radio.

fourteen

TOMMIE MOORER WAITED IN A BRIGHT ROOM WITH WHITE WALLS at the Jasonville Police Department. It seemed like a junior high principal's office. *This*, he realized, *is what telling your mother the truth gets you.*

"They say the truth will set you free," Van had once told him, "but all it ends up freeing you from is the things you'd rather be doing."

They had asked Tommie to come down and just answer some questions. But the questioning was beginning to seem more like an interrogation. Did they honestly think he had something to do with the murders?

Agent Ben Zane from the Indiana Bureau of Investigation came back into the room and attempted a smile. "So tell me one more time, after you stole the moped—"

"I didn't *steal* it, I brought it back."

"According to your uncle—"

"My uncle *knows* I sometimes borrow it."

"That's not exactly what he told us."

Tommie groaned. *Why didn't I follow my brother's advice?*

"Well I'm glad you guys found the 'stolen' moped."

"Watch it, young man," said Agent Zane. He downed his coffee and crushed the foam cup, then tossed it into a trash can by the wall.

Tommie stared back. *What? Like that's hard to do.*

Agent Zane sat down.

"Was it parked in Ned's shed?" Tommie asked him. "Like it *always is* after I'm done riding it?"

"Don't get smart with me."

"Would you rather have me be dumber? I can do that, you know."

"Cool it, son."

"There are plenty of examples to follow here," Tommie added.

The agent chuckled and got up from his seat, the scooting noise of his chair echoing obnoxiously throughout the enclosed room.

"Look, son…" Agent Zane began, and Tommie knew to tune out whatever lecture was coming next. Whether it was the school principal, a cop, a social worker, or a wanna-be step-dad, the story was usually the same. "Kid, I used to be just like you." They all use the same line, almost like they'd rehearsed it together. It worked zero percent of the time, but he kept that fact to himself.

"So you told your mother you saw someone out on the lake that night. That true?"

"Maybe."

Agent Zane's smile went away. "All right, cut the tough-guy act, kid. Did you see someone or didn't you?"

"I…" Tommie glanced at the door. "I mean *maybe* it was a person. It was dark."

"That's not what your mother told us."

Tommie didn't respond to that.

The agent made a tsk-tsk noise. "Well Tommie, I don't know what to believe."

"You think I'm lying?"

"Maybe."

"You think I had something to do with killing those girls?"

"I don't know." Agent Zane stared at Tommie. "But you seem a little uncomfortable."

Tommie said nothing. He drummed on the table with his fingers.

"You talk to me awhile," Agent Zane added, "maybe I'll figure out why."

Tommie looked at the door again. "Can I talk to my mom?"

Agent Zane smiled and nodded toward the door. "Yes, shortly. You really want to leave, don't you?"

"I just want to see my mom."

"Well, she *asked* us to talk to you *first*, then together if you both want. Regardless, you don't need to worry. In a couple minutes you'll be free to go."

Agent Zane flipped through his notes. "Hey, speaking of your mother, you aren't an only child, are you?"

Tommie felt a knot in his stomach. "I have a brother," he mumbled.

"Right," Agent Zane pointed as if Tommie had answered correctly on some TV game show. He pulled some photos out of a large, manila envelope, then placed one down in front of Tommie. "Do you recognize this person?"

The photo was several years old and showed a group of boys in soccer gear. Tommie didn't recognize the face Agent Zane was pointing to. He shook his head.

"Are you sure?" the agent tried.

"I'm sure."

"His name is Cameron Ford."

Tommie stared back. The name rang a bell, and one he didn't like.

"What about this person?" Agent Zane's hand had been covering up the face of the boy standing next to Cameron Ford—probably on purpose Tommie now realized.

He saw who it was and tried not to react.

"Let me ask again, do you recognize this individual?"

There were five boys in the picture, but only one next to Cameron, who was to the far right of the group.

His brother, Van.

The shot looked like a team victory hug, but Tommie realized that wasn't the point. Van had his arm on Cameron's shoulder.

"My brother played soccer with a lot of different kids."

"Sure. Of course. But now I'm curious, Tommie, who taught you how to ride a moped?"

Tommie hesitated. "My uncle."

"That's not what he told—"

"Fine, it was my brother who taught me how to ride! So what? He's *not* here. He's gone because of people like you!"

"Slow down, son."

"I'm not your son! I don't have a dad."

"Okay, okay, Tommie. Now, please, think with me a minute. Your mother's probably told you, hasn't she, that Van spends one weekend a month in minimum security?"

"No."

"Sure you rode out to Lake Lenape alone?"

"Yes."

"Haven't seen your brother recently?"

"No!"

"Okay then." Agent Zane abruptly switched gears, "Tommie, why are you so afraid to tell us what you saw that night?"

"I—"

"Look, we know *you* didn't do anything."

The agent leaned forward and Tommie got a whiff of his coffee-and-doughnut breath.

Tommie glared back and replayed the guy's last statement in his mind. And right then and there, he made up his mind not to tell the cops anything else.

Guy Redmond rushed into Greene County General Hospital.

He looked around hurriedly and didn't see his wife anywhere. He whipped out his cell phone.

"Sir, you can't use that in here," came a voice.

Guy spun around. A heavyset redhead in blue scrubs glared back. She pointed at a sign that served notice that all cell phone use was prohibited on the premises.

"Oh, uh...I'm sorry...I need to find my wife, Mikki Redmond. I got a message...I was in Chicago...our...our daughter was attacked...brought to the emergency room. My wife called. I need to talk to her. I need to find her, please."

"Sir, what is your daughter's name?"

"Hope. Hope Redmond."

The nurse acted uncertain, distracted. She looked at a chart and flipped a page. "Okay, yes, she was admitted."

"Yes, yes, is she okay?"

"Please sign in, have a seat, and someone will be out to talk with you in a moment."

"Ma'am, I—"

"We'll be right with you."

"I—"

"Sir, please sign in and have a seat."

He looked around the waiting room, still expecting to see his wife, but she was not one of the four people present.

Reluctantly, he sat down.

Guy let his eyes roam around the empty seats, the magazines and newspapers on the table. He realized he'd been holding his breath. He exhaled slowly, then drew in a big gulp of air, which smelled like elderly people and antiseptics. His mind began to whirl with scattered thoughts.

What am I supposed to do? Read a magazine?

"Mr. Redmond?"

He looked up and saw a woman—a doctor, or a physician's assistant maybe—in a stiff white lab coat. She didn't look much older than his daughter.

"Yes, I'm Guy Redmond. Hope's father. Is she all right?"

"Mr. Redmond, I'm Dr. Barnes," she reached out to shake his hand, "one of the emergency physicians. Your daughter is stable."

"What do you mean 'stable?'"

Dr. Barnes hesitated. "Mr. Redmond, you have no idea what's happened, do you?"

"I was in Chicago…my wife just called and said Hope was in the hospital…said she didn't have time to explain… just said to get here." He searched around again, expecting Mikki to appear.

"Your wife, yes. She came in to see Hope and fainted, but she's all right. I'll take you to her. And you can see your daughter, too. But you should know that Hope is very weak. She probably won't be able to talk. She was attacked by someone and stabbed in the shoulder, buttocks, and leg."

"Oh, my…oh…please *no*."

"Your daughter lost a lot of blood, and she went into shock."

"How?" Guy staggered. "How could this have happened?"

"The police have arrested someone. I don't know much more."

"Not *my* Hope."

"Mr. Redmond, do you know your daughter's blood type?"

"What?" Guy stared at the doctor blankly. "No. I mean, we have five kids."

"It's type O negative," Dr. Barnes replied.

"So, what's that mean? You still helped her, right? Gave her whatever she needed."

"Well yes, but it took a little longer than we would have liked."

"What! Why?"

"Well you should know that O negative blood creates a rare challenge for us, Mr. Redmond. An O negative person like your daughter can only receive O negative blood."

Guy recoiled.

The doctor spoke matter-of-factly. "Hope's treatment was delayed for several hours while we had to wait for blood to arrive from Terre Haute."

fifteen

MONDAY MORNING, STUNNED POCKETS OF MURMURING students formed a crowd outside Jasonville High.

Classes had been canceled, but by mid-morning the school had become an informal gathering place for those who hadn't gotten the message, the curious, and those who had to come because they simply couldn't believe what had happened.

Casey's eyes wandered across the school's landscape and parking lot. He watched as a group of girls on the school's lawn huddled around someone who was sobbing uncontrollably. Over by the smoking wall, another group of classmates had gathered to talk, heads down. No one had a cigarette.

Nearby, the school's sign still announced that Yellow-jacket T-shirts were on sale in the office. Next to it, a cluster of underclassmen was huddled together, murmuring quietly. Over by the bushes in front of the school's main entrance, one of the freshman teachers consoled another circle of girls. Casey saw universal shock and grief on every face. The scene was surreal, unlike anything he'd ever witnessed.

A few of his classmates had stopped by only briefly, but most, like Casey and his group from the Order, couldn't seem to get back in their cars and leave just yet. They stood in the parking lot.

"I heard they're bringing in some of the counselors who talked with people after Columbine," said Jeremiah, gesturing toward the school.

Everyone was silent.

"Like that's going to do anything," Mark finally commented.

Casey looked again at the crying girl. He thought she was an underclassman, but wasn't certain of her name. He was pretty sure she wouldn't have been friends with any of the victims, but the tears were definitely genuine.

"You never know," Casey whispered. "Look at everyone."

"Well, not like it's going to bring any of them back," said Jeremiah.

Casey looked at him. Jeremiah's eyes were glazed over. Casey realized his probably were too. Everyone's were.

"This place will never be the same," Mark said softly.

A cardinal trilled and swooped by. Someone in a green Mazda exited the parking lot. A couple of the guys sighed.

"Yeah, nothing they do is going to bring those girls back," said Jeremiah, staring toward the school.

"Or get Hope out of the hospital," added Casey.

"Or get Cameron out of jail," said Jeremiah.

The group stared at Jeremiah. He'd uttered the name they'd all been thinking of but were afraid to mention. No one said anything for a moment.

"What in the world was Cam thinking?" asked Mark, not really meaning it as a question.

Again, the group was silent.

"Anyone seen Neal?" Casey asked.

Just then, Danny and Eric walked up. Danny nodded solemnly toward the group. "Gentlemen."

"Hey guys," mumbled Casey.

"Unbelievable," Eric said, taking in the scene. "Just unbelievable."

"I can't believe that Cameron…" Danny trailed off. "Did any of you guys know he was going to do this?"

No one replied.

Jeremiah broke the silence. "Man, all I said was that I didn't like Claire. Not that I truly wanted her dead."

"And I certainly didn't mean what I said about Karen," added Casey.

Danny held up his hands. "Guys, we need to just chill."

"No one even remembers who picked who, anyway," said Mark.

"We just need to keep our mouths shut," Eric said.

"No problem there," Jeremiah replied.

A pair of non-Order students walked by and the group grew quiet. They stared back at the school.

"Cameron's in deep," Danny said. "There's nothing we can do about that."

Mark spoke up, "Hey, maybe we c—"

"Yo." Jeremiah nudged Mark and pointed. The group watched as Neal's silver Camaro pulled into the parking lot and headed their way.

"Everyone be cool," said Casey.

Neal stopped and got out of the Camaro and walked over toward them, anguish clearly evident on his face.

Nobody said a word. They all just stared at each other.

"Hey, man," Jeremiah finally said.

"Hey," replied Neal. He panned the group, then gazed toward the school.

"Bro, we are so sorry," said Casey. He thought about hugging Neal but didn't know if that would fly. Even here, even now.

Neal moved toward Casey, almost to the center of the group. He paused and smiled bitterly. "Not all of you are."

"What?" asked Mark.

In a blur, Neal turned and lunged toward Danny, grabbing him, slamming him backward into a car.

"Whoa, knock it off!" someone shouted.

"Not again."

Several of the guys moved in to break things up.

Jeremiah put his hand on Neal's shoulder and waved the rest of the group back. "Neal, buddy, this ain't helpin' things."

Neal had his forearm across Danny's throat. Danny winced but stood his ground. He seemed more worried about the scene than about Neal roughing him up.

"You put him up to it, didn't you?" Neal said.

"No."

"You told Cameron to kill her!"

"No." Danny replied, "No *way*."

"You…you picked Trisha…*you*."

Danny shook his head. "I *did not* tell him to kill Trisha. Or Karen. Or Hope. Or *any* of those girls. *This was Cameron's idea.* Remember who asked the question? *Cameron,* man. You think I'm happy about what happened?"

Neal seemed uncertain what to do next. Casey shot a glance across the school grounds to see if they were attracting any attention.

Nothing…yet. People kept talking in their clusters—mourning, grieving, wondering why. Any other day they'd be gawking.

Neal relaxed his grip a bit and put his head down.

Danny pulled Neal's hand off. "*Cameron,*" he said again. "Your issues are with Cameron."

Jeremiah tried to ease Neal away.

"Yeah, just like Jeremiah here didn't *tell* Cameron to kill Claire," Danny said.

Jeremiah paused. "Right."

Neal gazed up again at Danny, then at everyone. His body trembled and he still looked like he could burst at any moment. He stayed in Danny's face.

"We need to drop this," said Eric. "People are going to start asking questions."

"That's right," added Mark.

Casey's head was spinning from all the craziness of the past thirty-six hours. Other-worldly acids churned deep in his gut. For an odd, brief moment, he found himself missing Cameron, waiting for Cameron's leadership to help ease the situation. Waiting for something that would never come.

"Let's keep it together, guys," Casey said. "We *all* need to keep it together, especially now." He put his hand on Neal's other shoulder. "Neal, my man, I'm so sorry. We'll help you get through this."

A car pulled up behind the group from the opposite side of the parking lot, the sound of tires against concrete easing to a stop. They all turned.

It was a police car. A lady cop got out and asked, "Everything all right here, boys?"

"Yes ma'am," Mark replied. "We're cool."

Neal stared at Danny face to face one more time.

"*Cameron*," Danny said. "Remember who asked the question." He lowered his voice. "Remember it."

"Yeah. I got it," Neal said and turned away. He gestured to the group. "Thanks, guys." Neal headed toward his Camaro.

"Dude, I'll go with you," Jeremiah quickly said under his breath.

The cop spoke again, "Do you gentlemen know where I can find a young man named Casey Wood?"

No one responded right away. The officer looked like she was about to repeat the question.

"I'm Casey Wood," replied Casey finally. He didn't know what else to say. He felt a bit uncomfortable being called out like this, in front of everyone.

"Mr. Wood, my name is Deputy Lorraine Barrett with the Jasonville Police. I'd like to ask you a few questions."

"Let's get going," Mark said to the group.

Jeremiah and Neal were already pulling out.

"Okay, later man," said Eric.

Danny stretched his neck and collected himself. "Okay, see you guys."

"Later dog," said Mark.

Casey walked slowly toward the cop, growing more uneasy with each step. He glanced back and saw the guys watching him. Mark was staring with wide eyes. Other groups of students were also looking, some pointing, some nudging the person next to them. In fact, there was no one who *wasn't* staring at him.

AGENT ZANE HAD HAD ENOUGH OF TOMMIE. HE GOT UP TO LEAVE, but instructed Tommie to wait.

Some older guy came in and introduced himself as Agent Rodney Jergens. Tommie waited for Agent Zane to leave, but that wasn't going to happen.

Two against one. Tommie was up to it.

"My colleague tells me you saw someone out at the lake the night of the murders," began Agent Jergens, not letting Tommie correct him. The agent plopped some new photos on the table. "Now were either of these the person you saw?"

Tommie studied the pictures and saw three faces. One was Van, one was a mug shot of Cameron Ford, and the last was some older kid Tommie didn't know.

"Sure ain't this one." Tommie took the picture of Van, then Frisbee-tossed it on the floor.

The agents looked annoyed.

"But like I said, it was dark. It might not've even been a guy."

"C'mon kid, come clean here and nothing's gonna happen to you," said Agent Zane.

"What about these other two pictures?" Agent Jergens pressed.

Tommie stared at the photos. He took the picture of the kid he didn't recognize and set it aside. He looked at the photo of Cameron.

Agent Jergens stepped forward. "Is that him?" he asked. Agent Zane seemed to close in a bit too.

Tommie couldn't speak. There was a buzzing in his ears. Why wouldn't the agents just leave him alone? Tommie blinked and flashed back to his experience at the lake.

The figure.

The darkness.

That puke feeling in his gut.

Tommie's eyes started to water. He glanced at the picture and shook his head. "No," he replied.

Agent Zane sighed—that kind someone does when they'd really prefer to swear—and ran his hands through his hair.

Agent Jergens wrote something down.

"At least...I can't be sure," Tommie said.

"C'mon kid," prodded Agent Zane. "Go with your instincts. You hesitated on that last picture."

"The person I saw," Tommie stopped and shook his head.

"It'll be so much easier if you'd just tell us," Agent Zane coached.

Tommie grimaced.

Agent Jergens couldn't take it. *"What?"*

Finally, Tommie looked Jergens in the eye. "I can't tell you who it was."

"Why?"

"He had a mask on, genius."

Lorraine sized up the young man as he walked. She noticed some uncomfortable body language and his steps were measured, cautious. He kept glancing back. Those things might not mean anything, of course—what with people staring and all.

Casey Wood wasn't short nor was he tall, and he had a medium build. He wore a blue jacket with a maroon stripe, blue jeans, and a pair of charcoal-gray Nikes. He was a good-looking boy with trim dark hair and big blue eyes. The kid's face and the way he walked reminded her a little of Frodo Baggins. Or at least the actor who'd played him.

Casey stopped and stared at the squad car.

"Mr. Wood, would you mind telling me where you were last Friday night?"

"This about what happened to Hope?"

Lorraine smiled. "If you don't mind, please just answer the question."

Casey sighed. "I was at a friend's house, Mark Craver's, with a bunch of guys until pretty late, maybe 11:00," he said, sounding like he'd given his account several times already. "Then, I went over to another friend's house until after midnight. On my way home I found Hope."

"And Mr. Craver and your friends can verify this?"

"Yeah," Casey turned toward the school. "Actually you could've asked them before they took off." He smiled ever so briefly. Almost the perfect combination of nerdy innocence and cool.

Lorraine smiled back and nodded. "Oh, we'll talk to them soon, I'm sure."

"Is that it?" Casey asked. "I'd like to get going."

"No, not quite. So you were at Mr. Craver's until around 11:00 on Friday? And who, again, was the second friend's house?"

Casey's face squirmed a little. "A girl's."

"A girl?"

"A girl whose parents didn't know I was over. And I still don't want them to know."

"Care to offer a name?"

"Why does it matter?"

"Again, I'll ask the questions. Miss Redmond's maybe?"

"No!" said Casey, like she was the stupidest person on the planet. "I *just* told you I found her later."

"Yeah, let me ask you something about that. After you found Miss Redmond, what did you do?"

"I tried to get her to calm down, to tell me what happened. She said she'd been stabbed, that someone was after her. A woman came to the door of the house and asked what was wrong, then I told Hope to go inside and call for help."

"And then?"

"What do you mean?"

"Did you wait for the police and ambulance to arrive to tell them what happened?"

"No."

Lorraine acted surprised. "Why?"

Casey stared at her a moment, his eyes focused. He had naturally long eyelashes that most women would give anything to have. Lorraine quickly chided herself for noticing a detail like that under the circumstances.

"I went looking for him," he explained, sounding a bit shaken. "I thought I saw something, some movement, so I went to check it out. I thought he may still have been chasing after—"

Lorraine interrupted, "Why not wait in the house with the women?"

"I wanted to go after—"

"So you, weaponless, charged out after a killer, after learning that he'd stabbed someone?"

"I...I just. The look on Hope's face."

"The woman, Mrs. Marchete, said you ran off pretty quickly."

They stared at each other.

"I went after the scum who stabbed Hope," Casey responded firmly. "Where were you?"

Lorraine held her composure. "It was a tough night for all of us. As you know there were five other crime scenes we were called to. We did catch your friend Cameron though, as you may have heard."

"He's not my friend anymore," replied Casey, emotionless.

Lorraine paused a moment and found herself believing that much at least.

"Well, that's good," she replied. "He's in a lot of trouble."

"May I go now?" asked Casey.

"Did Cameron Ford ever discuss anything with you that would make you think he intended to do something like this?"

The kid hesitated just a moment too long. "No."

"Okay, so did you find anything when you went looking for Miss Redmond's attacker?"

"No."

"How hard did you look?"

"As hard as I could, in the dark, without a flashlight or anything. I ran around for a few blocks, looking for any sign of him. Everything was quiet, dark, like any other night. I wasn't thinking about time, and when I got back to that house, Hope's ambulance was just leaving."

"But you didn't stick around to give the police a statement."

"Look, no, I mean, I was exhausted. Or maybe I got scared. Sorry, I don't have a lot of practice with that kind of situation. Maybe I made a mistake."

Lorraine gazed at the school and thought that comment over a moment. She decided to gamble. "Well, all told, it's a good thing the ambulance got there when it did. A few more minutes and Miss Redmond might not have made it. As it is, she's still really struggling."

Casey's look became hollow. "She was in pretty bad shape."

"She's still at Greene County General in Linton," Lorraine continued. "She lost a lot of blood, as you can imagine. The hospital thought they'd stabilized her with transfusions, but she's taken a turn for the worse."

That got the kid's attention. "*What?*"

Lorraine knew she was in breach of confidentiality rules, but felt it was worth the risk. Her instincts told her that if there was more to the kid's actions that night than simply trying to help the Redmond girl, this might be the only way to find out. She couldn't really envision the parents suing her, or Rix coming down too hard.

Casey grimaced and put his hand to his face. "What happened?"

"Don't know for sure. They aren't certain what the

problem is. She's still in the hospital, Mr. Wood. They're doing everything they can."

There was a pause.

"I really need to go," Casey said softly. His blue eyes seemed misty.

Lorraine tried again, "Tell me who you were with before you found Miss Redmond?"

Casey looked sad. "Why does it matter?"

"What if I told you a witness reported seeing someone matching your description outside *earlier* in the evening than you say you were out?"

"Someone's mistaken," Casey replied, perhaps a little too quickly.

In the nearly vacant parking lot, cop and high-school kid just looked at each other for what seemed like a long time.

Finally Lorraine spoke, "Thank you for your time, Mr. Wood. You have a good day."

Tommie gazed through the window of his mom's station wagon and was glad to see the Jasonville Police Department getting farther away.

The agents had let him go after murmuring something to his mother about "keeping in touch."

Tommie was bothered by some of the things they'd asked him. Of course, nearly everything he'd told them back at the station *was* technically true.

But Tommie knew a secret.

Cameron woke up from a brief, uncomfortable nap to the sound of shoes walking down the hall. He hated trying to sleep in this place, this tiny, bunk-bedded jail cell. Why wouldn't they ever turn off the lights and let him get some sleep?

Every time he'd feel ready to doze off for good, he'd roll over and sense red warmth just outside his eyelids. He really hated it at night—the always-on lights. No one had ever told him that about jail.

Someone stopped next to Cameron's cell and pulled up a chair. Cameron sat up in his bunk and rubbed his eyes.

"Mr. Ford?" A graying old man in his fifties—sixties maybe—peered in the cell.

"Uh, there anyone else in here?" Cameron asked.

"No, you're the only one here." The old man smiled. "My name is Miles Ashton. I'm a chaplain from Bloomington."

Cameron stared. "A what?"

"A chaplain, with the prison system. We provide spiritual counsel to inmates."

"Oh." Cameron grimaced. "Like a minister or something."

Chaplain Ashton smiled again. "I am a reverend, but that's not the point. I'm not here to preach you a sermon."

Cameron did not reply.

"You might not be aware, but Indiana is one of the few states that offers a specific religious program for inmates. I work primarily in a segregated housing unit for prisoners who've volunteered to participate."

"Whatever."

Chaplain Ashton studied him. "Well, Mr. Ford, Cameron—may I call you Cameron?"

Cameron slowly nodded.

"It seems you could use a friend right now."

There was a pause. Chaplain Ashton gazed at the bars.

Cameron sighed. "*You* wanna be friends with me? Right."

"Well, Cameron, anything you tell me is confidential."

"I haven't talked to the police. Why would I talk to you?"

"My purpose is different. I'm here to listen to you, pray with you, or offer you guidance in any way."

Cameron laughed. "You know, that's nice. Really. But you're wasting your time."

Chaplain Ashton's face wore a knowing expression, like

he'd expected as much. "Son, are you familiar with God's holy Scriptures?"

"What?"

"The Bible?"

"Oh yeah...heard of it."

Chaplain Ashton smiled again. "Do you know any of the stories?" he asked.

Cameron shrugged his shoulders.

"Did you know that great men like Moses and the Apostle Paul, for instance, were murderers who God forgave—"

"But I'm *not* a murderer, Reverend. I didn't kill anyone."

"What?" That seemed to throw Chaplain Ashton off. "Well, as I said, Cameron, anything we talk about is confidential and—"

Cameron stood up and pointed. "I just said I *didn't* kill anyone!"

There was silence as they stared at each other.

Chaplain Ashton's face now held sorrow. "Cameron."

"Yeah, I know I shouldn't yell at you like that." Cameron sat back down just as a deputy leaned into the hallway and looked at them. "Like I said. You're wasting your time with me."

Chaplain Ashton stood and picked up the chair. "I'll be back to see you again in a couple of days. If you decide you want to hear about Moses or Paul, or if you have any questions, I'll be glad to spend some more time with you."

As the chaplain walked out, a thought hit Cameron for the first time.

He was utterly *alone*, and he had no one to thank but himself.

sixteen

KEVIN FINISHED REVIEWING HIS NOTES ON HIS MACBOOK PRO, then used the motel phone to call the *Tribune*.

"O'Malley."

"Andrew, it's Kevin."

"Hey, whatcha got for me?"

"Not sure yet. I've talked to a few people."

"Yeah?"

"What if there's nothing new to be found?" Kevin said, trying to lower the expectation bar—and maybe also persuade himself there was truly nothing here.

"You'll find something. What about the kid's parents?"

Kevin clicked and opened a file on his laptop. "Mr. and Mrs. Edward Ford. Late forties. Married. Stable. No affairs. No controversy. He works at the IGA grocery store. She's a substitute teacher. They have an older daughter who's married."

"We can start there. You know: 'Kid's background runs counter to strong family ties.'"

"Yeah, great."

O'Malley asked, "Has anyone recognized you yet?"

"Not that I know of."

"Just remember that for every person who despises you, someone loves you."

"Not sure you've got your ratios quite right," Kevin replied, "but that's a lovely thought."

"I hear it often. You still have fans."

"Sure," Kevin mumbled.

"So what's Jasonville like?"

Kevin did not reply.

"Gibson?"

Another moment passed.

"You all right?"

No, I'm a thirty-one-year-old pro with a bad vibe from a foggy cornfield. He realized how odd it might sound.

"Yeah, fine. I'll call you, Andrew."

"Great."

Kevin hung up. Stretching the truth with O'Malley was nothing new, but something was bothering him. He closed the laptop.

Fear. It was the four-letter "F-word" no investigative reporter should have in his vocabulary.

Either there was something here, or he was really turning into a pansy.

He wasn't sure which one he liked less.

CAUTION, BERTRAND RIX THOUGHT AS HIS HEART RATE ROSE. *Proceed with extreme caution.*

He stared across the conference table at Greene County Prosecutor Merrill Cross. Rix had wanted to bring one of his deputies to the meeting to balance things out—a suggestion Cross had knocked down. Rix was beginning to see why.

Cross had done a fine job making sure the deck was stacked in his favor. Gathered for the briefing were Greene County Sheriff Judd Graham, agents Rodney Jergens and Ben Zane from the Indiana Bureau of Investigation, Cross, and Rix.

"Gentlemen, now," Cross began, gesturing toward Zane and Jergens. "Lay it out for me once again so that even the densest jury in the state would want him put away. Spare no details."

"He's eighteen," Jergens replied, "and I think we have the goods to lock him up until he's at least sixty."

"Sixty?" asked Zane. "You're being generous."

"Do share," said Cross.

Jergens nodded at Zane. "You go ahead. You always tell it better than I do."

Zane opened a file and started reading.

"Hope Redmond was stabbed in the shoulder, buttock, and lower leg, all on her left side, by a butcher knife with a seven-inch blade. The knife, the same one later used to stab Bertrand in the shoulder, was recovered during a search of Tyre's Tomb."

Rix grimaced.

"What about the blood evidence?" Cross chirped.

"We found both Rix's blood and the Redmond girl's on the knife, as well as on the clothing of Cameron Ford."

Jergens raised his eyebrows. "See, Ben here doesn't miss a thing."

Cross sighed. "Go on."

"Although weapons were not found at the crime scenes for Beth Simmons, Geena Wolford, Claire Borden, Karen Gothman, and Trisha Geller, we're still searching alleys, water drains, and Dumpsters. Our theory is that Cameron Ford disposed of the weapons as he went along on his killing spree, and that he still had the butcher knife only because he encountered Chief Rix as he was fleeing from his attack on the Redmond girl.

"Executing a state-issued court order, we seized a collection of videos—including six *Friday the 13th* movies—and other horror movie paraphernalia from Cameron Ford's bedroom. We also recovered a number of clothing items and other weapons that we're running further tests on. We've learned that Cameron Ford is right-handed, and the medical examiner indicates that at least three of the other victims were killed by a right-handed individual.

"There are eight corroborating witness statements—not bad for a town with one zip code—of sightings from either late Friday or early Saturday of a young man in a paintball mask, in each instance matching the height and build of Cameron Ford.

"Last but not least, we have the statement of the seventh person attacked that evening, who just so happens to be the chief of police, who can testify to chasing down, overpowering, and arresting one Cameron Ford."

"Forty to fifty years minimum," proclaimed Jergens, "if not life."

Zane flipped through the last few pages of the file, then folded it shut and nodded.

Rix thought Zane might have even winked across the table.

"Well?" said Sheriff Graham, turning to Cross.

Cross rubbed his chin and revealed a hint of a smile. Everyone but Rix seemed to want a group high-five. The atmosphere oozed with a heavy pre-prosecution vibe, like a three-beer buzz readying them for the most high-profile—possibly career-defining—case of their lives. It was happy hour for the ready-fire-*aim* crowd, and someone else was buying.

Rix, and *only* Rix, it seemed, was concerned with other issues.

The timeline bothered him. As did the fact that Cameron Ford's car had been parked in his driveway and not on some Jasonville street. How did the kid get around so quickly? Sure, Jasonville was small, but there were limits. And where did Cameron stash all the murder weapons, only one of which had been recovered? How did he carry them all, if not in his car?

Then there was the Geller residence garage. Blood, fresh blood, found in the garage didn't match Trisha Geller's. Nor could it be matched to Cameron Ford. No one in the room seemed bothered or even interested.

"We file by week's end," said Cross. "Five counts of first degree murder, two counts of attempted murder."

"All too easy," said Zane.

"Not bad for a few days' hard work," added Jergens.

Rix stood up abruptly.

"Bertrand?" Sheriff Graham called after him.

But Rix ignored him. He was already out the door.

CHAPLAIN ASHTON RETURNED FOR ANOTHER VISIT. "AS PROMISED, I'm back," he said, nodding.

"What day is it?" asked Cameron.

"Wednesday."

"Oh." Cameron glanced away. "Seems like...longer."

The chaplain reached through the bars and handed Cameron a book. "I've marked some parts I think you'll find of interest."

Cameron paid him no attention. "Okay."

"Aren't you even going to look at what I gave you?" asked the chaplain.

"Let's see, chaplains are like reverends. A chaplain gave me a book. Let me guess: it's a Bible," said Cameron.

Chaplain Ashton smiled. "Would you be willing to look at something with me?"

Cameron hesitated before responding. "You're wasting your time with me. But yeah, I'll humor you. Kinda hard to waste any of my time right now." He flipped open the book. "What?"

"Son, did you know that the largest book in the Bible is a book called 'Psalms?'"

If the chaplain was looking for some reaction, Cameron wasn't going to give him one.

"It's near the middle," Chaplain Ashton said.

Cameron flipped pages as slowly as possible.

"Would you turn to Psalm 146, verse seven—verses are like lines, by the way—and read me what it says?"

Cameron gave a half-smile. "You don't know?"

Chaplain Ashton was silent a second, then slid his chair back a little. "You're humoring me, remember? You've got time."

Cameron flipped the last few pages as non-gently as he

could, and the sound echoed down the hall. "Seven, you said?"

"Yes, 146, verse seven. Actually the third line of verse seven."

Cameron read, "The Lord frees the prisoners."

"Good," said Chaplain Ashton.

Cameron looked up from the book and toward the chaplain. "It's that simple, huh?"

"Yes and no," replied Chaplain Ashton.

"Sorry, man I'm a little slow here. You're gonna have to help me with this religious stuff. If that's true, and you're the Lord's rep, then tell me: when do I leave?"

"The Lord *can* free you, if you let him, Cameron. But you have to ask yourself: What would being free mean?"

Cameron shook his head and spoke softly, "What?"

"Let me show you. There's a sticky note in the front," said Chaplain Ashton. "What's the first line I wrote down?"

Cameron hesitated, then opened the front of the book. "Romans 3:23."

"Turn there and tell me what you find. It's past Psalms, a bit further through the book."

A moment later Cameron found it. "And?"

"Read it and see if that answers your question," Chaplain Ashton responded. "Start a verse before, at twenty-two, if you can."

Cameron read, "We are made right in God's sight when we trust in Jesus Christ to take away our sins. And we all can be saved in this same way, no matter who we are or what we have done. For all have sinned; all fall short of God's glorious standard."

Chaplain Ashton smiled. "Skip forward and read twenty-five, too. It's important."

"For God sent Jesus to take the punishment..." Cameron paused and glanced skeptically through the bars. "For our sins and to satisfy God's anger against us. We are made right..."

"Go on," Chaplain Ashton prodded.

"...with God when we believe that Jesus shed his blood, sacrificing his life for us." Cameron held the book open, gazing at it like something wasn't right. The cell was silent a moment.

"What does that mean to you?" asked the chaplain.

"It means," Cameron looked around his cell as if another person was somehow going to appear, "that everyone can... well...no, there's no way. I mean, that's not what I've always believed. Not how I was raised. There's no way. Can't be."

"God *will* set you free, Cameron. It's simply up to you."

"No."

"Don't take my word for it, Cameron. What do the words you just read tell you?"

"I see what it *says*. You and I are no different. But you might not believe that if you knew the things I've done." Cameron looked the chaplain in the eye. "Actually...I know you wouldn't."

Idiots.

Rix walked away from the meeting room as quickly as he could. His first instinct was to go home, but instead headed down the hall toward the cells.

He stopped. Something—level-headedness, maybe... hopefully—kept him from going any farther. He stood still.

Then he also remembered the chaplain might still be there visiting, so he kept his distance. Still, a part of Rix wished he could confront all the nonsense and just drag the Ford kid down to the meeting and get everything straight. Course then it would become an issue of rights, real and imagined, and lawyers and posturing and egos.

Rix glanced in the direction of the meeting room. No one else had come out yet. He knew he needed to speak with Cross alone, even though it might not go anywhere. For sure, he wasn't going to get anywhere if Zane and Jergens were around.

He looked back toward the kid's cell.

Questions. Maybes. There were still so many of those and that bothered him.

"It's not how I view you, or how you view yourself," said Chaplain Ashton. "It's what God says."

"You think you know," said Cameron, scowling. "But you don't."

"Cameron, I—"

"Just flat out *don't.*"

"Okay then, tell me. What makes us so different?"

Cameron paused, then laughed. "Well if you have to ask…how many people have *you* stabbed in your life, Chaplain?"

"Son, what makes you think I've never been on the other side of these bars before?"

Cameron was silent.

Chaplain Ashton leaned forward. "Last time I was here, you yelled at me that you were innocent. Now that we're talking about God letting you off the hook, suddenly you've done too many bad things."

"I…" Cameron began. "Just forget it." He shook his head.

"No matter who we are or what we have done," said Chaplain Ashton, pointing toward the book Cameron still held. "You read it yourself."

Cameron clenched his jaw. "That's too good to be true. Besides, look at me." He threw up his hands and beheld the cell, letting the chaplain do the same. "Doesn't God have better things to do? Better people to worry about?"

"Cameron—"

"I'm a complete mess." He dropped the Bible on the floor, a thud echoing through the whole cell block.

"Cameron, listen. God doesn't expect you to clean up your act and follow him. He wants you to follow him and let *him* clean you up. Religion is from the outside in. Christ works from the inside out."

Cameron thought for a moment. "You still don't get it, do you?"

Chaplain Ashton said nothing.

"I'm evil," said Cameron.

"That's a lie."

Cameron scoffed.

"It's an adjective. It's not your true identity."

Cameron stared. "How can you argue with that?"

"I'll always argue with evil. But you know what I won't argue with?"

"No," replied Cameron, disgusted. "What?" He looked away.

"Love," said Chaplain Ashton.

"I wish I had a clue what you're talking about," Cameron said. "I don't."

"Search your heart, Cameron. I think you do. God gave us a planet of creative splendor, but he didn't just stop there. He gave us a face. Somewhere we could see love. A human face."

"Whatever."

"But you've seen it, Cameron. And you will again." Chaplain Ashton smiled. "It's your mom, feeding you as a baby and worrying every time you cried. It's the woman you haven't met yet who'll one day be your wife, looking at you from across a crowded room. It's a dad picking up his daughter after she's fallen off her bike. It's a nun playing a guitar in the street, smiling at a young lady whose soul is tormented by some dark secret. It's your grandmother on her deathbed, looking at you with caring eyes. And she speaks the words, 'My child, remember when you used to read to me?' and you sense it in the room with you— something bigger than yourself. Something holy." Chaplain Ashton nodded. "Love."

Cameron buried his face in his hands, held still.

After a minute, Chaplain Ashton stood. "You know what, I'll leave the book here with you. We can talk again in a few days."

Cameron looked up. "See ya," he whispered.

Chaplain Ashton turned and walked away, his footsteps gradually fading out down the empty hall.

seventeen

BERTRAND RIX STEPPED OUTSIDE THE POLICE STATION TO GET some air, and thought he detected the distinct smell of menthol and tobacco.

He located the culprit loitering not far away from the building: Chaplain Miles Ashton.

Rix cleared his throat. "You know, God may forgive, but smoking doesn't."

Chaplain Ashton smiled and let out a puff, "You said it."

"How have you been, Chaplain?"

Chaplain Miles Ashton looked a little more gray than the last time Rix had seen him. But his demeanor still had a grace to it, even puffing on a cigarette.

"Great, Chief. Yourself?"

Rix gazed off across the street, toward Shakamak State Bank, and didn't answer. Instead he said, "Doesn't smoking set a bad example in your line of work?"

"Perhaps," said Chaplain Ashton, "But if I toss it down on the ground with you watching, that's littering."

"Correct."

"And if I throw it in the trash, I'm one step away from being an arsonist."

"You can't win," said Rix.

"I can't win."

A big, loud-engined panel truck roared past the station, and Rix eyed the driver, who slowed a bit. Some squirrels in a nearby tree broke into a chatter that sounded a lot like an argument.

Rix asked, "So why did you come all the way out here?"

"It's a nice drive," the chaplain said. "And the people here like me. You, for instance."

"We only have one inmate."

"Is that right?"

"Does God like it when you're not forthcoming with people who ask you questions?"

"Depends on the people."

Rix raised his eyebrows. "What about people who have earthly authority?"

"Hmm, I don't know. I'll be sure to ask."

Rix changed gears. "We haven't seen you down here in awhile."

"Yeah, I've been busy up north. Indiana's been on the cutting edge ever since the legislature passed that initiative for inmates who volunteer for religious training."

"Right, heard about that," Rix replied. "Didn't realize you were involved."

"Well we've got three special prisons now, with separate housing for men, women, and juveniles," the chaplain said. "Keeps me in demand."

"And yet you managed to extract yourself to come down to Jasonville?"

"I heard about the case on the news. Figured no one would come around until...unless he got sent up to the state pen."

"Understood," Rix said. "It's good to see you again. People in town are really searching for answers right now."

"Well, my role is pretty much limited to what I can do in there," the chaplain said, gesturing toward the police station.

"But you've been around town a bit. What do you think— we ever coming back from this one?"

The chaplain shrugged. "I heard you got stabbed. How's the shoulder?"

"It's fine. And don't change the subject."

"Let me put it this way, Chief. Remember the weeks right after 9/11? Churches were crowded, filled with seekers looking for spiritual truths. Groups were organizing candlelight prayer vigils. That was then. People forget and move on. They stop being so afraid of their mortality." The chaplain gazed at his cigarette.

Rix smiled briefly. He noticed the mayor's parking space was empty.

"But what if we get it wrong here?" Rix nodded toward the station.

A pair of kids came out of the bank laughing hard at something, their mom hurrying after them.

The chaplain cocked his head. "You seem like you're trying to ask me something, Chief Rix, without really asking it."

"Am I?"

"Aren't you?"

"Like what?"

"Maybe something about what I discussed with your inmate today?"

"No."

"What a relief," said the chaplain. "For a moment, I was worried. I know you're a professional."

"Indeed. You, too."

"Then what's on your mind? Shoot straight with me."

Rix stared at him. "You gonna be back again soon?"

Chaplain Ashton smiled. "That almost didn't sound like a question."

"Yeah, I guess it *almost* wasn't," Rix replied.

They were interrupted by a holler of "Chief!"

Rix glanced up and saw Deputy Barrett standing halfway out the door with an urgent look on her face. "Greene County's on the line for you."

"Tell 'em I'll be right there," Rix shouted back.

"Merrill Cross?" the chaplain asked.

Rix didn't answer.

Deputy Barrett headed back inside and the door closed.

"Nice chatting with you. Don't keep yourself so scarce." Rix headed in to take his call.

Chaplain Ashton chucked his cigarette and let it bounce across the pavement.

eighteen

"She had to go *back* to the hospital?" Casey asked.

Hope's Aunt Maria stood in the Redmonds' doorway Friday afternoon and nodded solemnly.

"Why?"

"She came home yesterday and seemed to be doing fine, but then she started getting feverish and complaining about her shoulder hurting worse and worse."

Casey shook his head. "No," he mumbled.

"She got very dizzy and we rushed her back. The hospital said she must have gotten an infection in her shoulder that spread. They were pumping her full of antibiotics, but there were...*toxins*. I don't understand everything about it, but I guess the toxins and medications negate each other at first. It may take awhile."

"I thought she was going to be okay. *Damn*."

"Hope's dad had to leave, but her mother is with her."

Casey regained his composure. "Excuse my language. I'm really very, very sorry to hear that. I...I had no idea. Thanks for telling me, Maria. I know that this must be tough on all of you."

He turned and walked hastily to his car. As the front door closed, he drove off with a squeal.

Deputy Barrett watched Casey Wood's car go tearing off. She radioed in.

"Yeah, he just took off. Want me to keep tailin'?"

She drummed her fingers on the wheel as she awaited instructions.

"Okay. Whatever you want."

Lorraine pulled out and headed down the street in the opposite direction.

TOMMIE MOORER WAS OUT IN FRONT OF HIS HOUSE MESSING around with his skateboard when the police car drove by.

As it slowed and the cop looked at him, Tommie put his head down and skated the other direction.

The police car kept going.

He let out a breath.

It had all started because Tommie told the truth about a robbery Van and his friends had pulled. His mom had been grilling him about where he'd gotten certain things, did he steal them, and so on. He'd ratted out his brother, who'd given Tommie some cool stuff. He'd blabbed the truth to his mother, who got all worried about the stolen merchandise and tried to make things right with the cops. Just like that, boom, Van was gone. Now, Tommie might as well be an only child. Lesson learned. He knew he couldn't trust the cops. Van never had.

He still missed his brother. He remembered his mother bawling so hard the day they took Van away. Eight months ago, but it felt like forever.

Tommie had been in the backyard, trying to blow up a pencil eraser with a firecracker when he'd heard the shouting from the front of the house. Tommie had run through the back door and seen the cops through the hall on the front steps. They grabbed and arrested Van, right there in the driveway, making a big show of things for all the neighborhood to see. Van had tried to run, but some big man tackled him. Tommie's mom kept shouting "No," but no one had helped.

People still looked at Tommie funny—the kid brother of that "bad" kid.

Why would he ever help the cops anyway?

The truth just wasn't worth the risk. To his brother and also, maybe, to himself.

He skidded the skateboard to a stop and looked back. The police car was well out of sight. He picked up the board.

Tommie knew a secret. And he wasn't planning on sharing.

He'd lied about the lake.

There'd been no mask. He'd actually only heard about that part—the killer supposedly wearing a mask—on the news.

Tommie had, in fact, seen a face.

WHEN RIX ARRIVED AT SHEILA'S STEAKHOUSE, GREENE COUNTY Prosecutor Merrill Cross was already seated for dinner.

"Chief Rix, great to see you," said Cross, rising. "Wine's on the way. Hope you like Zinfandel."

"Thanks." Rix sat down, noting that Cross was eyeing him closely.

Sheila's Steakhouse bounced with the ting of silverware and plates. The smell of well-seasoned, grilled beef and honey barbecue wafted through the air. People chatted at nearby tables, absorbed in their own realities.

"You look good these days, Bertrand," said Cross. "Wife keeping your carbs down?"

Rix sighed. "I'm not going to sugarcoat this, Merrill. I'm concerned about the Ford case."

"Really? How so?"

The waiter came over and poured them both a drink. Cross ordered a sirloin and baked potato. Rix went for the ribs, even though his stomach didn't feel right.

"I think you know."

Cross launched into a spiel about moral obligations, community, laws that could actually be enforced, and doing the right thing even when it was hard, even when it hurt. The speech was full of all the right catchphrases, yet came across as amazingly unimpassioned and shallow. Rix had heard stuff like this for years. Whether in meetings or conference calls, it all sounded the same. He took a sip of his wine and waited for Cross to finish.

"You know you aren't running for office here, right? You don't have to feed me that."

"That's why I'm feeding you dinner, too." Cross smiled. "Besides, you're a voter, aren't you?"

Under normal circumstances, Rix might have smiled in return. Instead, he shook his head.

The waiter brought them bread.

When he left Cross said, "For crying out loud, can we just eat?"

Rix stared at him. "I know you want to file five counts. Quite frankly, I'm not comfortable with that."

"Why do you say that?"

"I think you know why."

"Sheriff Graham feels comfortable with the charges."

"No offense, but Judd wasn't there."

Cross put down the bread he'd been gnawing on. "I presume you're trying to make some point here, Bertrand. I just can't tell what it is."

"Let me put it this way, Merrill. I'm your only *bona fide* witness."

"Right, you got stabbed. All the more reason—"

"It's more than that and you know it. Or *should* know by now."

"What I do know is that you're a team player, and testifying against Cameron Ford is the right thing to—" Cross's cell phone rang. He muttered a self-important "excuse me" and took the call.

Rix sighed. He saw his meal coming and decided to make do.

When Cross got off the phone he didn't say anything. He went for his dinner.

For the time being, the pair ate in silence.

Jasonville was in an uproar, and Rix was having ribs, courtesy of the taxpayers. Man, did he feel weary. Things hadn't always been this way.

He'd studied criminal justice at Indiana University in Bloomington. A Dean's List student and member of Delta Tau Delta. He'd played tight end at a college that worshipped basketball and viewed the football program as nice window dressing. Back in his twenties, he could run a pretty mean flag pattern.

His foot speed had come in handy during police training, a livelihood that became a foregone conclusion after he'd met his wife, Melinda. She'd demanded some stability and wanted to settle down, yet she was willing to meet him halfway. Poof, like that, his destiny was to become a small-town cop.

Rix had worked stints in a number of forgettable places before landing in Jasonville. That was twelve years ago, and while it was good to be chief, the work took its toll.

When he considered the cost some of his peers had paid, Rix counted his blessings and knew he was lucky to still be married to the same woman.

Over the years, the crimes had gone from graffiti to guns (though never much gun*fire*, which was good), from shoplifting to car theft, from kids ringing doorbells to assault. The culture was in a slide, no doubt about it. Pundits would debate the reasons why. Didn't matter. Cops like Rix didn't take sides.

He'd never had that great of a relationship with any of the county prosecutors, and Cross was no exception. It was hard to accept. Most of them treated crimes in Jasonville like they were some sideshow on the way to true greatness.

Well, the real show had arrived. And some of the good guys were on the verge of screwing it up. Badly.

Cross spoke, "You know, usually small-town police chiefs want to crack some heads. When given the chance, they really want criminals to suffer their wrath. I don't see that desire in you."

"Yeah? And?"

"C'mon, Bertrand, humor me."

Rix ignored the dig and asked, "What about the blood in the Geller garage?"

"What about it?"

"Have you done anything else about trying to match it?"

"People get cut in garages. It's not that rare."

"So the evidence we collected doesn't matter to you?"

"Find me a case where everything matches up perfectly, and I'll show you a case where human beings weren't involved."

Rix decided he didn't care if the ribs got cold. "With all due respect, Mr. Prosecutor, that's a cop-out and you know it."

"*Look,*" Cross began, "I'm trying really hard here to not tell you where to go. You aren't making it easy. What do you want me to say?"

Other restaurant patrons were now starting to cast glances their way.

"That you won't file against Cameron Ford until we find out more. And that you'll at least review the blood again."

Cross stopped cutting his potato and stared at Rix a long time. "Bertrand, how many multiple-homicide cases have you ever worked in your career?" he asked.

Rix listened to the murmuring of people, the tink and clang of forks and steak knives.

He realized there was one, and only one, outcome they were heading toward before this conversation ever occurred. And there would be one—the same misguided one—after.

"And look who I brought with me this time," said Cameron's mom.

Cameron smiled at his sister and niece. He'd never heard his mom like this, sounding so grandmotherly.

When his mother came to visit, they let him out of his cell for a while, which was good, though a deputy always stayed close by.

"Hi, Emily," Cameron said to his sister. "And hello-o-o, baby Laura."

"Hey, little brother," Emily said. "How ya doing?"

"I'm okay," Cameron lied.

"Emily insisted on coming to see you."

"Just call me Uncle Cam."

Mom and Sis laughed, and it was nice to hear.

Cameron's mom spoke, "You know, your sister is handling things like a pro. You'd think she's been a mom for years."

"That's great," Cameron said.

There were more smiles and laughs. It was the first time he'd seen his niece, and he couldn't help being happy for Emily. Seeing a newborn baby with cell bars in the background was a surreal experience. He wouldn't have guessed there would be anything that could upstage jail.

They talked—mostly his mom talked—about her job, Emily's GI hubby, the baby, the new family car, breastfeeding, the weather, and more.

Cameron glanced over at the deputy, hoping he'd fallen asleep or something. No such luck. He was sure the visitation time was winding down. Then the baby cried.

The sound jarred Cameron. Maybe he was just too used to the solitude of jail, but…

She cried more.

Louder.

His niece sure could get up there in decibels. He looked at his mom. She just kept on *talking*.

Didn't this bother anyone else?

He looked at the baby. She seemed peaceful, but he still heard crying.

Louder, still.

Stop. Please stop.

The noise was in his eardrums, pounding its way through his head.

Cameron tried to get his sister's attention. "Can...can you..."

She was oblivious.

The sound pierced, wailed. Louder and louder and louder.

Then, he realized. Baby Laura was *calling to him*.

Cameron's eyes bounced around the room. The deputy looked bored, unaware.

The sound felt like it was flattening him.

What's happening to me?

More crying children joined Baby Laura, layering over each other.

This can't be real.

He was sure he could hear them though. He blinked, then shook his head.

Finally, his mother looked at him, concerned. "Cameron?" she mouthed, but he couldn't speak.

Another baby, sounding like it was suffering some unspeakable terror, then another. The voices piled on, all screaming, wailing.

A fourth, a fifth, a sixth, a seventh, an eighth, a ninth.

An unstoppable force, they came. Like the piercing clamor of chimes. The screaming cries. Fading in, unbelievably loud. Another coming on top of the one before.

The voices grew older. One shrieked in his left ear, another blared in his right. Pain, unrelenting. Tormented human cries. Voices in front of him and behind. Suffering. Deathly.

Cameron was breathing heavy.

The sounds. Like all the suffering in the world converging in one place. Coming after him.

"Stop!" he shouted toward his sister and baby Laura.

His sister stared back horrified.

"Make it *stop!*"

Cameron was shaking in his chair. His face felt hot, his skin crawled with a burning sensation.

He could hear teenage girls screaming, then adults.

"No!" he screamed back.

The exploding cries continued.

"No!" he screamed again, his voice cracking, his throat raw.

No mercy, the screams taunted him. Cameron's body heaved. He pulled on his chair. He pulled away.

"GET...ME...OUT...OF...HERE!"

His sister stood, recoiling at the sight of him. His mother was also standing, reaching for him.

Baby Laura cried out to him.

The deputy stood.

Cameron collapsed to the floor.

The deputy tried to pick him up.

"*No!*" Cameron exploded, fighting, but not really against the deputy.

Two more cops responded to the commotion.

They yelled at him, but he couldn't make out anything.

The voices...still.

The cops hauled him out of the room.

nineteen

At 8:30 A.M. on Saturday, Kevin headed out of his room. The motel office was open, and he could see someone was actually at the counter.

He gave his shirt a sniff and stepped into the doorway. The office was a mess, with papers everywhere. A window air conditioner that looked like it hadn't cooled anything since the Carter Administration sat on the floor next to the counter. A gray-haired woman in black-rimmed glasses stood behind the counter, the closest thing to a manager he was going to find.

"Hi. My name's Kevin; we met the other day. I'm in room eight."

"Yes?"

"I meant to ask, are all of the rooms here 'smoking?'"

She seemed to be thinking hard. She cleared her throat. "People don't have to smoke in the rooms if they don't want."

Kevin's mouth fell open a bit, but he reined it in.

The woman was serious.

"Oh, all right."

She nodded. "Sure."

Kevin tried to give a polite smile.

He turned and headed for the car.

This must be a lot like hell.

"The cops are breathing down my neck," Casey told Mark, as the two sat at Mark's kitchen table.

"Weird. Why?"

"They don't seem to like my alibi."

"Why would you need an alibi? Cameron's in jail."

"Yeah. I don't know. I think they're…"

"What?"

"I guess I really don't know."

"What did you tell them?" Mark asked.

"Well they seem extremely interested in what I was doing at Ashley's. Like that matters. Anyone could've found Hope. I was trying to leave Ashley's name out of it, but they aren't making it easy."

"Why don't you just tell them you were over there?"

Casey hesitated. "Her parents were gone. I wasn't supposed to be over."

"So?"

Casey did not reply. He knew his being over at Ashley's had nothing to do with the horror that happened later that night. But he still felt awkward.

Mark smiled. "Ohhhh. I think I see what's going on here."

As he drove around Jasonville, Kevin observed the layout of the town: Dollar General store, a Cassandra's Pizza, the IGA grocery store, and two gas stations. Jasonville also had quite a few churches, especially for a town of only 2,500 people. There was a single fast food option for the entire community. Naturally, the Subway in Jasonville didn't accept credit cards. Most places in town frowned on plastic. He'd discovered that one the hard way.

Most of the houses in Jasonville had a green newspaper box for the *Linton Daily World*, a publication he'd never heard of that seemed to be the preferred local paper. DirecTV and Dish Network were also popular. A massive, powder-blue water tower near the middle of town proclaimed Jasonville to be the "Gateway to Shakamak." Shakamak was the name of a state park three miles west of town. It was apparently home to three lakes, Lenape being the most popular. He might have to check it out.

"Shakamak State Park, three miles west on Highway 48." Periodically Kevin supported his mental notes by speaking into a digital recorder, a nifty *Tribune*-bought gadget with a USB port to download MP3 files. "Remember to visit tomorrow."

He set the recorder aside and reflected a moment. Sometimes he missed the brainless excitement of athletic competition—simple drama that even drunk people in sports bars could understand. But investigative work gave him the ultimate challenge: Uncover something shocking. And if that proved impossible, at least uncover something people hadn't already heard.

Yeesh.

He continued driving and made a discovery. Jasonville was an Indiana Historic Site. He spoke into the mic. "First nighttime high school football game in Indiana history. Jasonville over Jasper Academy, 20–0, on November 17, 1928." Kevin glanced up at the lights installed above the field and wondered if they were the same ones.

Two blocks past the historic site, an unmarked car occupied a spot designated as "Police Parking Only" outside the building that housed the Mayor's Office and the Police Department. There did not appear to be any Visitor Parking, so Kevin drove on. He'd have to stop by at some point and introduce himself.

Across the street from the police station sat the Shakamak State Bank. Kevin smiled. *Well at least the bank should be safe.*

That reminded him of something. "According to the locals, there aren't many robberies in Jasonville. But the town has had some issues with crime from time to time. Though certainly nothing that compared to the recent night of carnage."

Obviously there wasn't a whole lot to do in Jasonville. Two young ladies who worked at Subway had told him about one favorite young male activity around town. It consisted of throwing beer and an old couch in the back of a truck, "cruising uptown," and then sitting on the couch, drinking, waiting for interested girls to happen by. Yeah baby, Romeo would be proud.

Kevin noticed very few media types left around town. If there was anything more to the story than what others had already reported, at least he was in the right place to find it.

He raised the recorder to speak again and saw the display: "Low Bat." When had it quit on him? Had it recorded anything today? He tossed the recorder onto the passenger seat.

Kevin had an extra pair of Duracells in his bag, but to get it he'd need to go back to his motel room, and its distinct, lung-cancer-scented sheets.

Every so often, though it was becoming rarer, Velma Moorer could *tell* when something was up with her son Tommie—when something was bothering him.

Since returning from the police station he'd resembled a scared rabbit, twitching and looking around, expecting some unknown, bad thing to happen.

His demeanor spoke volumes to her. Velma had seen similar behavior before. Both her ex and her older son had displayed the same troubling tics.

Tommie was sprawled out on the couch playing video games.

His talents at lying to her frightened her sometimes. Like his claim he'd been totally straight with the police.

It was disturbing how much like his older brother little Tommie was becoming. They might as well have named him Van, Jr. As a mother she knew, somewhere deep down, she'd blown it with Van. She'd ignored moments like these.

She wasn't going to let that happen again.

Velma would have to play Mean Mom if necessary. Deny

him the things he liked—no video games, TV, telephone, internet, skateboard, time with friends, even his favorite foods—until she got the truth. The real story about what happened to Tommie out at the lake, not the hooey he'd fed the police.

She would have to risk him running away. It would take some determination. But a breakthrough would be worth any anguish. She needed to know. A lot was riding on the outcome.

Tommie was ignoring her. But she had a plan.

Under the door to his room, Kevin made his most interesting discovery.

A note.

He opened it:

YOU LIKE TO INVESTIGATE?

DID YOU KNOW THAT A CORPSE
LOSES FIVE POUNDS A DAY,

WHEN LEFT IN A CORNFIELD?

HAVE FUN ASSHOLE.

Bertrand Rix called Deputy Barrett into his office.

"Lorraine, remind me who Tommie Moorer is?"

"Uh, I think that's the kid who was out driving around on a moped the night of the murders."

"Who interviewed him?"

"Let me think...Zane maybe? Yeah, it was Zane from IBI."

"Where's Zane's report on that interview?"

The deputy gave a blank look. "Good question."

He smiled at her. In a way, he felt sorry for Deputy

Lorraine Barrett. He was barely managing to cope with everything that had happened. And usually, he was the strong one. Everyone had their breaking point. Wilkins had actually shed tears that night. And Hayes had vomited at the Geller crime scene.

Lorraine was one pretty tough chick. Or at least she played the part pretty well. The stereotype led some in Jasonville to cast doubt upon her orientation, spread rumors, and all that lovely small-town stuff. In reality, his deputy was more likely to be seen around town helping a cat out of a tree than involved in anything salacious. She was single, had short hair, and wasn't particularly attractive. In fact, Rix knew that was probably why his wife let it slide…him having a female next-in-command and all that.

She was better at getting information out of certain people. From working in other places, Rix knew the gender thing could cut both ways. But Lorraine was a good fit for what he faced in Jasonville. Course he'd never dealt with anything like this. How could he ever "staff up" for multiple homicide?

Answer: He couldn't.

"Find that file for me," he said to her.

"Done, Chief."

"And then would you check into this *Friday the 13th* business?"

"What?" She shot him a puzzled look. "Why?"

"Because *we* investigate, cover all the bases. Greene County prosecutes." He rapped on the desk. "If I don't cover it, Murphy's Law dictates that Cross will ask me about it."

"You got it."

KEVIN WAS DRIVING, SEARCHING, TRYING TO DEDUCE WHICH FIELD the note writer had in mind. His mind drifted back to the cornfield he'd passed on the way to Jasonville. *No. Too far out of town.*

But there was a cornfield just outside of town to the

northeast, past the green and white "Jasonville" sign.

A white graveled parking lot for Spalding Baptist Church bordered the cornfield to the east. Kevin pulled in.

There was a huge pole in front of the church with the American flag hanging from it. Just outside the entrance stood a lone, aged tree on the lawn, making the place appear a bit like Minas Tirith from the last *Lord of the Rings* movie.

Kevin stared at the church and the cornfield. *A corpse loses five pounds a day when left in a cornfield.*

Was the note a hoax, or had some congregational conflict escalated from cantankerous to extreme?

He parked and stepped out of the car. There were several things that bothered him, but he focused on two: One, who'd left him the note? Sure, he'd spoken with a few people already—people who could have told others about his questions. And there was only one motel in Jasonville. But still.

Two, what was its purpose? Obviously, whoever left it wasn't interested in helping his investigation. Some people got off on hoaxes. Maybe this was one. Maybe there was something more to it.

He walked to the edge of the cornfield. As he stood there, gazing at ten-foot-high cornstalks, another question occurred to him.

Was he being watched?

He felt that way, even though no one was letting their presence be known.

Historically, there came a point in certain cases where he could rationalize almost anything. He'd ask himself: If he risked it all, including his life, who would it really bother? Certainly not the paper. His mother, maybe. That was it.

Because the investigation was always king, he was accustomed to proceeding with conduct a normal person would consider blatant stupidity. He was wary, but confident he could handle himself, regardless of the situation.

He looked over at the church. There were no cars in the lot except his, no signs of activity.

"Hello?" he called out. It was silly, but it sounded better than, *Would you please show me where the corpse is so I don't have to search this entire field?*

No one said "hello" back.

Of course he might be in the wrong cornfield. He turned and headed for the Tiburon.

He fired up the engine and headed out of the parking lot. A sign in blue letters greeted him, as it would greet all those exiting the lot: "Take Christ to the World."

Kevin caught something in the rearview mirror.

What the–?

He turned the vehicle around and drove toward the cornfield, crawling to the edge where gravel met soil. He got out.

The person was no longer there. Cornstalks swayed in the breeze.

Kevin put his hands on his hips. He was either seeing things, or he had, in fact, spotted a masked figure standing just outside of the cornfield.

twenty

KEVIN STOOD STILL, DEFIANT.

He gazed along the edge of the field. The rows of corn went on for hundreds of yards.

About fifty rows down, a masked figure emerged.

He stared.

The masked face stared back.

He was tall, almost certainly male, young it seemed, and well-built. He wore a dark paintball mask that looked like a villainous costume prop from a *Star Wars* movie.

The masked young man waved Kevin toward him.

Kevin recoiled. "What?" he mumbled.

The guy pointed in his direction, then waved again. Kevin couldn't tell if it was a "bring it on" wave, or something less hostile. It didn't really matter. There was no way in the world he could afford to walk away from this empty-handed.

He stepped forward.

The kid disappeared into the corn.

CHIEF RIX HAD ZANE'S REPORT ON HIS DESK.

It was, as Rix had guessed, merely a synopsis, with very few direct quotes. Though this was common practice in police reports, self-absorbed IBI agents like Zane typically achieved an even greater level of brevity. Probably covering his own penchant for ticking off witnesses.

Rix flipped through the pages.

In the real world—not the one people see on *Cold Case Files*—witness interviews were rarely recorded. Unless a witness made the transition to true confessor, investigators were left with only written reports to review.

Still, there were some things in the report of Tommie Moorer's interview with Zane—and later, Agent Jergens—that bothered Rix.

Maybe if he drank another cup of coffee, he'd figure out why.

KEVIN CONSIDERED THE FACT THAT HE WASN'T ARMED. HE stared at the spot where the masked kid had been. People had been killed in Jasonville, and heading in unarmed was at best unwise, at worst, suicidal. Then again...

Someone's already behind bars for those murders.

Kevin was hesitating and didn't like it.

How bad could this be? It was a cornfield in the middle of Indiana, not some Middle East war zone like some of his colleagues had survived. Investigative reporters didn't get to call for backup.

He heard the stalks rustling a few feet ahead. He headed in.

"Hey, wait."

Kevin couldn't see Mask Guy. The noise he was making sounded like it was only a few yards ahead, so Kevin followed.

The sounds stopped. Kevin tried to get a fix on the guy, but the corn was too tall.

"Hey!" he shouted, "What do you want? What am I supposed to see out here?"

A flock of crows flew by. The sound of cornstalks being snapped came from somewhere much farther off than before. Kevin stood still. He heard and saw no further movement. Was he being ditched?

"Hey!"

Kevin turned around. He wasn't sure exactly how deep

he was into the field, but he thought he knew which way he had come.

"All right, I'm leaving!"

Mask Guy appeared to be gone for good.

Kevin headed back toward his car, listening every few feet, and doing something else: *smelling*. He'd heard from crime victims and law enforcement friends that the stench of human death is unmistakable, even from many yards away. If the note writer had his facts straight, and the Mask Guy had led him to the right field, there should be, well, other indications.

Kevin's senses picked up on nothing. He felt a degree of relief. Of course he wanted the story and all, but some things were better left experienced secondhand.

He glimpsed the top of the church between the stalks, and congratulated himself on his navigational skills. *Kevin Gibson: Human GPS.*

A figure came into view, standing at the end of Kevin's exit row.

Mask Guy was back. Kevin was getting annoyed by his game.

Brazen punk.

Only it wasn't the same Mask Guy.

This kid wore a blood-red colored paintball mask, and he had cornhusk hair dangling from the lower chin of the mask. He stood in an I-dare-you-to-get-past-me pose.

Either the first guy had changed masks or…

Not good.

Kevin turned and went the other way.

And there was Mask Guy number one, waiting—countering Kevin's maneuver—and angrily shoving cornstalks out of the way.

Extremely not good.

Kevin veered to the left.

Five feet away from him was yet another pursuer in a paintball mask. This one was a white Greedo from hell, with ridges along the mask's neckline that resembled gills.

Kevin yelled and ducked to the right, sprinting, smashing through cornstalks, cringing as stalks whipped into his face, stumbling as he came across the raised dirt of the field's rows.

He heard his pursuers doing the same. Cornstalks cracked and smacked and gave way.

Which direction?

He couldn't see where he was heading. The rows were too tall. He had no time to think, to plan, to strategize. He sprinted and stumbled, sprinted and stumbled.

Still coming.

Kevin had no idea where he was in the field until he saw it: a pivot road running down the middle of the field. Kevin came out into the open.

He reached for the only "protection" he had, his cell phone.

The LCD mocked him: "No Service."

Whap! Kevin felt something pop in the middle of his chest, then searing pain. He stumbled back and into the rows of corn. Instinctively he put his hand to his chest and felt the wetness. Kevin recoiled and stared back at…

Bright pink.

What?

A paintball.

Whap! He got hit again, this time in the right shoulder. He screamed in pain, stumbled, and started to run.

They shot him in the back, at least three hits, all stunningly painful. More shots connected as he tried to zigzag away. Each collided against his body with sudden, stinging force, like bullets might do if they couldn't pierce skin.

The rounds came in a torrent, and they stung like nothing he'd ever endured. He'd lost his sense of direction. He jumped and tried to see above the corn.

All he could see was corn. Corn that went on and on and on and on.

They fired unrelentingly. The guns made a horrible, forced-air popping sound that echoed all around him.

A shot nailed an ear of corn right by him, splattering paint in his eyes. He shouted in pain.

Kevin took one in the jaw.

It felt like a musket round. He fell to the ground and held his face. A tart, chemical-infested taste assaulted his tongue. Kevin spit violently.

The shots continued to land all around him.

"Enough!"

Some of the paintballs hit his body but didn't break open. And they hurt even worse.

Pieces of corn leaves rained down on him, while the relentless popping above shredded nearly everything. He began to army crawl across the rows.

That appeared to work—temporarily throwing them off their game. He heard them shouting at each other. Male voices, definitely young.

The paint in his eyes burned terribly. And he could feel nasty welts forming all over his body.

Like most people, Kevin had only seen paintballs in sporting goods stores. What he had never imagined was how badly the gumball-sized bullets hurt.

The field grew quiet. Kevin eased up to one knee, peering through the stalks and for any foreign color. Out of the corner of his right eye, he saw white. Kevin dove face-down and got dirt in his mouth to add to the paint.

When he peered up, he saw another clearing up ahead. He snuck toward it.

No luck. He'd gone in a circle—or perhaps an oval—and was back at the pivot road again. This time considerably deeper into the field. The road was his sure ticket out, but if he was caught in the open he'd only take more shots.

The white flash he'd seen was a bulk chemical storage tank, perhaps ten feet long, sitting on the back of a boat trailer. On the side of the tank in large letters were the words "AMMONIUM NITRATE." A thought popped into his mental LexisNexus: *Timothy McVeigh.* Kevin's eyes drifted to the tank's red "Combustible" warning diamond.

Should he bolt or wait it out? So far his decisions had only brought trouble. He needed to *not* make another mistake.

Think!

Two minutes of silence passed with no shots or voices. As quietly as he could, Kevin stood up and scanned. He couldn't see anything but corn. Which way was his car?

He propped himself up on the tank on all fours. Ever so slowly, he rose and stood. He could see the entirety of the massive field.

He couldn't spot the car, but he saw the church. It didn't seem that far away, which was a pleasant surprise. He tried to calculate which row would be the best one to follow straight down and out...

Something moved.

Lines emerged in the corn. Two, then three. All moving. Closing in on him.

Kevin winced.

He tried to step too quickly and slipped off the curved edge.

"No!"

Kevin landed on the ground with a sickening thud, his back twisted up against the tank, facing the clearing.

Just as Mask Guy number one, the fiendish, insolent kid in black, emerged from the corn.

Saturday afternoon Casey received a call from Jeremiah Bronson.

"Hey, my friend." Casey hadn't talked to Jeremiah much since the Order had stopped getting together after the murders. He hoped the unofficial hiatus was temporary, but he had his doubts.

Jeremiah jumped right in. "Neal's bad," he said, and Casey could hear the strain.

"How bad?"

"Like, 'I don't have any reason to live' bad."

Casey felt a lump in his throat. "Where is he now?"

"I think home."

"Okay, what should we do?"

"Well, dude, I hate to drop this on you, but that's just the thing. I don't want him to be alone. His parents aren't taking things much better than he is. But I have to go up to Terre Haute with my family today. Maybe you could go hang out with him awhile?"

"Yeah, of course. That would be good."

"And maybe take Mark along, too, or one of the other guys."

"We'll do it."

"I think you guys hanging out with him awhile might do Neal some good."

"I'm there. Thanks, Jeremiah."

One by one, Red Mask, Black Mask, and Greedo stepped out of the field and joined each other on the pivot road.

Kevin held up his hands, like people do on TV whenever real guns are being pointed at them.

Black Mask had orange splatter on his goggles, apparently from friendly fire.

They came toward him.

"Guys, enough," Kevin said. "I've had enough."

Red Mask crept up the closest. Extra camouflaging from bits of corn husks made him truly hideous, almost satanic. He cocked his head and stared right through Kevin.

What kind of depraved mind was behind that mask?

They all stood above him, expressionless. All three masks had disturbing slashes, carvings in the plastic, on the nose and cheek areas, and oversized, inhuman eyes. Two of them had no mouth, the other had jagged slits.

Red Mask pulled out a long Rambo-style knife with a serrated back edge and brandished it in the Indiana sun.

Kevin caught his own reflection on the blade, up against the fertilizer tank, cornfield in the background. He screamed.

Red Mask paused, taking in the fear, then violently threw the knife down next to Kevin's leg with tremendous force. Kevin flinched.

Red Mask raised a gloved hand, pointed down the pivot road, and began a countdown from five on his fingers. The other two raised their guns.

Kevin didn't understand.

The countdown continued.

"RUN!" one of them hissed.

Kevin popped up and started to run.

He heard laughter and realized what was coming with sickening fear.

They started firing again, this time toward his feet.

Dirt flew up on both sides of his shoes. A paintball nailed his Achilles tendon, stinging him horribly and nearly making him fall.

"Stop!" he yelled, though he knew they wouldn't.

The paintballs continued to smack all around his feet, one striking the back of his left calf, another whacking him in the opposite ankle.

Kevin was exhausted. He didn't know how much farther he could go. He kept running, waiting for them to either decide enough was enough or run out of ammo.

He emerged from the cornfield just north of the church. He allowed himself a glance back. They were gone. He collapsed.

His body was covered with paint splatters and throbbed in more places than he could count. His once-white Reeboks were a revolting mess of yellow, orange, and pink, all mixed with dirt.

Kevin willed himself up and staggered to the Tiburon. He reached for the keys.

He couldn't find them. Frantically he started pulling out

his pockets. All he found was a room key to the Jasonville Motel.

He stared in horror back toward the cornfield.

twenty-one

CAMERON FELT GRUDGING RELIEF WHEN HE SAW CHAPLAIN Ashton outside his cell again. It was the day after Cameron had heard the horrifying screams. He wondered if the chaplain had been told about the incident.

"Why me?" Cameron asked without any small talk.

Chaplain Ashton hesitated a moment before replying. "Why *not* you?"

A door slammed somewhere in the jailhouse.

The chaplain beheld him with apparent pity. "Something bothering you?"

Cameron gripped the bars and sighed. "How do you do it?"

"I'm not sure what you mean."

He looked Chaplain Ashton in the eye. "How do you know all the things you seem to know?"

The chaplain smiled. "Well, let me answer that this way." He cleared his throat. "I think a clergyman in a G.K. Chesterton short story said it best, 'Has it never struck you that a man who does next to nothing but hear men's real sins is not likely to be wholly unaware of human evil?'"

"Hmm." Cameron nodded.

"And Hebrews 13:3 says, 'Remember those in prison as if you were their fellow prisoners.'"

"You seem to find it hard to answer my questions without using a Bible verse."

"That right?"

"Yeah. Maybe just once you could...you know... *deviate*."

"Okay, son."

"Let me ask you something, Chaplain. Does God...cause guilt?"

"Guilt?"

"Like stuff that happens in your mind."

"What do you mean, Cameron?"

"Voices."

Chaplain Ashton paused. "What kind of voices?"

Cameron stepped back and kept silent a moment. He didn't know how to say it. He stared ahead.

"Bad."

The chaplain almost smiled, which Cameron found disconcerting.

"Probably not."

"Probably?"

"Young man, I don't know everything. I can't speak for God. But from what I know of him...bad voices aren't his. He *does* nudge a man's conscience. He can set you onto the road toward repentance. But once he gets you there, he doesn't pile on condemnation."

"I'm not so sure," said Cameron. He felt an urge to scratch the back of his neck.

"Oh, I see," replied the chaplain. "I think I understand what you're really asking. Let me answer it this way: God's voice and Satan's voice can sometimes come one right after the other, usually with competing messages. Sometimes they talk right over each other. The truth is the dividing line. Remember what we read?" Chaplain Ashton pointed toward the Bible he'd given Cameron, on the floor next to the bed. "The truth sets you free. 'You're guilty' is one message; 'you're doomed to hell' is quite another. Never believe the latter."

Cameron stood silent. Then he coughed.

"May I ask you something, Cameron?"

"Yeah?"

"When we first met, you told me you hadn't killed anyone. In fact, you were quite emphatic."

"Right. So?"

"So have you done something to invite *bad* voices?"

Cameron did not reply.

The chaplain took a pamphlet out of his pocket and slid it through the bars.

Cameron took it without a word and tossed it onto his bed. He ran his hand through his hair and stared straight ahead.

The chaplain stood up to leave. "When you are ready to reply honestly to that question, then I—and maybe God—can truly help you."

Greene County Prosecutor Merrill Cross was fond of the view from his second-floor office window. The office overlooked the courthouse grounds in Bloomfield, Indiana—the county seat. Bloomfield had roughly the same population as Jasonville, which was twenty-three miles to the west, and mattered more these days than at any time during his twelve-year tenure. Watching the two men in suits step out of the burgundy Lincoln and head up the steps of the County Courthouse & Administration building, chatting lightly as they walked, he enjoyed the perspective. He liked to see what was coming.

He swiveled the chair away from the window and back to his well-kept mahogany desk. He took a deep breath as he got up to welcome the visitors.

"Good to see you, Bob. What brings you out our way?"

Bob Marshall shook Cross's hand and gave him a sit-and-we'll-get-down-to-business look. Marshall introduced Cross to Dan Thompson, who followed closely on his heels.

"Have a seat, gentlemen."

Cross knew Marshall only socially, from mingling at various state functions. Marshall was a bigwig in Indiana state politics. Cross had never met Thompson, but he certainly knew of him. Thompson was a multi-millionaire business magnate, third generation in his family.

"I wish we were here just for a friendly chit-chat between fellow Republicans," Marshall began, "but there are a couple of important items that I need to discuss with you. One is personal, which I will get to in a moment. The other is political."

Thompson nodded along, as if Marshall was saying something of eternal significance.

"Okay, shoot," Cross replied.

"We have a situation out here in the eighth," Marshall deadpanned.

"Grossman's in deep," Thompson chimed in, almost sounding excited. "Too deep."

Cross sighed. *Grossman* was House Rep. William Grossman from Indiana's Eighth Congressional district. "How so?"

"His Chief of Staff is pregnant," said Marshall. "Yeah, he's got a little bundle of joy on the way, conceived with the wrong woman. She's going to resign next week. Word is, Grossman's poor wife has been attorney shopping. The whole thing's about to blow up in his face."

Cross was accustomed to hearing bad news, especially lately. He still winced.

Thompson glanced at his cell phone then spoke, "Two papers are sitting on the story, just biding their time. We've got a source. As soon as people start getting bored with what's happening down here, Grossman's going to be front page news."

"And?"

"He's gonna put us in trouble out here in the next election, unless we put the kibosh on it early and decisively."

"Bottom line on Grossman: he's *out,*" declared Marshall. "We're going to pull our support."

Cross let that sink in without enthusiasm. He'd voted for

Grossman twice and regretted the news, but he had more pressing concerns.

"Whatever happened to weathering the storm?" Cross asked the men. "This kind of thing is hardly unheard of in Washington."

"That approach might fly in some blue state, or D.C., but not in Indiana," said Thompson.

Cross couldn't really disagree. "So how can I assist you?"

Marshall nodded across the table. "Lots of people are looking to throw their support behind someone. We've been talking…taking some straw polls. You could be our man."

Cross sat up. "What?"

"It's a great opportunity for you, Merrill. A great honor," said Thompson, smiling. "Think of all the good you could do."

Marshall adopted a fatherly tone. "We know you're already keyed into running for public office. You won't be out of your element. And we'll make sure the state party gets behind you."

Thompson waxed eloquent, "Opportunities like this don't just fall out of the sky too often. You'd be crazy not to jump on this one."

"As you know, Dan here is my top adviser," Marshall continued, patting Thompson's shoulder. "You'll receive our full support and resources the other side only dreams of."

Cross protested, "But what about—"

"Fact is," Thompson cut in, "Grossman's ticked off some people and become a liability anyway. He's been giving us solutions for things that aren't problems ever since he got re-elected."

Marshall was checking out the view outside the window. Cross would have smiled under different circumstances.

"We're talking big donors. Movers and shakers. People who make things happen."

"Okay, gentlemen," Cross held up his hand. "Let's slow down here a minute."

That got Marshall's attention.

"What if I feel a responsibility to Greene County," said Cross, "to the people who elected me? I mean, I'm flattered by this kind of talk. Really. This may sound strange, but I get satisfaction out of being a prosecutor."

Dead silence.

A car door slammed outside. Marshall and Thompson exchanged a knowing glance.

"May I speak frankly here?" Marshall said.

"Please."

"Let's face it, Merrill. You're not getting any younger."

"This is an invitation to the big leagues we're talking about, without question," said Thompson. "Think about your legacy."

They paused for dramatic effect.

Cross realized he was in the middle of a coordinated game. And his career was the ball.

"Starting salaries in Congress are in the one-sixties," proclaimed Marshall.

"And you would not *believe* the freebies," Thompson added, "plus all the fringe benefits."

Marshall stood and asked, "Greene County has what, maybe 30,000 people?"

"Yes," Cross mumbled.

"We've got connections with the PR firm of Greer & Devereaux." Thompson spoke with a sparkle in his eye. "You say the magic word and they'll be on board."

"The eighth district," Marshall's cell phone rang, "covers nineteen counties, I believe." He flipped it open and stepped toward the door.

Cross overheard him say, "Yeah, we're still here. Come on up."

Thompson kept talking. "We time this right, and the state news cycle is going to spin from Jasonville, to Grossman's scandal, to the announcement of your candidacy.

Picture it, Merrill. A press conference on the steps of the state capitol announcing you as the next Congressman from District Eight. A cool banner in the background. We'll have Jasonville parents and key state party leaders singing your praises."

Marshall snapped his phone shut. "Only two conditions."

"I'm listening."

"One, you need to stay married. No diddling around if you get famous from your handsome mug being on the tube so much. We can't have another Grossman scandal."

"Of course."

"And two, you have to nail Cameron Ford to the wall."

"What?" Cross stared ahead.

"Remember when I said one of the reasons I was here was personal?" said Marshall.

"Yes, well…" Cross feigned a look of incredulity. "We're all taking it personally, Bob. My people and I are working hard on the case. Believe me, I'm prepared to go for it all. Why are you asking—"

A third man in a suit entered Cross's office, simply letting himself in. Marshall held up his hand for Cross to hold that thought, then murmured something to the newcomer.

"Prosecutor Cross," the man said, walking over to the desk and extending his hand, "my name is Raymond Simmons. I just drove over from Jasonville. I hear you're thinking about running for the House?"

"Glad to meet you." The name registered and Cross cringed inside, though he tried hard not to let it show as he shook hands. He suddenly remembered Chief Rix's questions about the case from their dinner.

"Ray is my brother-in-law," Marshall explained. "His daughter, Beth, was killed by Cameron Ford. She was my niece…for sixteen short years."

Marshall, Thompson, and Simmons were staring at Cross like they were fixing to pound him silly if he didn't say what they wanted to hear. Cross couldn't find the right words.

Simmons beat him to it. "And while we're speaking privately among friends, let's be real forthright here. He didn't just *kill* her. He took a hammer to the back of her head."

More silence.

"Yes," Cross whispered.

"As terrible as that was," Simmons continued, his voice cracking. He nodded at Marshall. "I'm not even asking for you to do anything that harsh to him, *Representative Cross*. I just want him to die. Lethal injection will suit me just fine."

Thompson stood. All three of them were now standing over Cross's desk. Cross kept still in his chair, trying to convince himself that Rix's doubts weren't the reason for his lack of enthusiasm.

"And if it's not too much trouble," Simmons added, "I'd like to be there to witness it."

twenty-two

KEVIN STOOD IN THE CHURCH PARKING LOT, SHOOTING GLANCES at the cornfield and at his car. He started as a black Toyota truck barreled into the parking lot. At first he thought it was there to run him over and put him out of his misery, but the driver ground to a stop right in front of him.

A young man leaned over and hollered at him, "Having car trouble, sir?" He raised his eyebrows when he saw Kevin's clothes, but all he asked next was, "Need a lift somewhere?"

Kevin squinted and put his hand up, trying to focus through the glare of the sun and the cloud of dust caused by the truck's abrupt halt—the kind you see when a driver is surprised...or in a hurry.

The driver had dark hair and a classic, struggling young-man moustache. Kevin was suspicious. He couldn't think of anything else to say, so he decided to reply with the truth and see what reaction it got, "Yeah, kind of."

"Okay then. Hop in."

Something wasn't right. It was too quick. Too convenient.

Kevin shot a quick glance over to the corn and saw nothing. *Just roll with it. There's something here.*

The young man smiled—and danged if he didn't look almost charming for a second—and opened the passenger door.

Then their eyes met and held a beat, and an image

slammed into Kevin's mind. Goggles...eyes...a red paintball mask...himself screaming.

"Name's Kevin. I appreciate the ride. I'm sorry—what was your name?

"Eric."

Ah, youth. Sometimes so cagey, sometimes so quick to speak.

"Thanks so much, Eric."

"Sure."

The truck sped out of the lot.

"H*EY*, *WHEN DID YOU GET THE PARKING STICKER*?" M*ARK ASKED* from the backseat, as he, Casey, and Neal rode in Casey's car out west of town.

"My dad splurged for it last month. Said I go to Lenape so much, it was cheaper this way."

"Lenape rocks," Mark declared.

"Thought we might throw the ball around a bit, see if we can't keep it out of the water." Casey pointed over his shoulder toward his duffel bag, which was sitting opposite Mark's feet. "You know, just for fun. Like old times."

"Right on," Mark said.

"Brought us some Mountain Dews in there, too."

"Soda. Wow, you shouldn't have."

Neal wasn't saying much.

"So whatchu think, man?" Casey asked him, "Colts gonna get it done again this year?"

"Don't know..." Neal gazed out toward the trees. "Don't really care."

They passed Lynch's Roller Rink, Engel's Self-Service Wood, and Shakamak Estates, driving deeper into the forested area approaching Shakamak State Park.

"Maybe on the way back, we can cruise by the old soccer field," said Casey.

Mark exchanged a knowing glance with him, then turned to Neal. "Field Jordan, baby!"

Neal replied without smiling. "The field is gone. Think they're trying to build a Wal-Mart there."

There was an awkward silence in the car. Casey and Mark glanced at each other.

Mark changed the subject. "Dude, what is this stuff we're listening to? Find another station, man."

Casey realized his radio had been playing a song by some *American Idol* goofball. He quickly turned it off. "Forget it, we're here."

They pulled in to the check-in gate, then drove down toward the water.

A dark brown sign proclaimed "Parking Prohibited Beyond This Point" in thick yellow letters. The dense trees—sycamores, maples, birches, oaks, willows, and pines—made it impossible to see the water, even though the spot where Casey parked was only feet from Lenape's shore. There were thick knee-high weeds and ample brush, all making one final effort to defy the change of fall.

Casey, Mark, and Neal walked down the curvy path. It was paved but narrow, with small wooden posts every few feet bordering both sides. They came to a sign that said "Road Ends in Water." Casey found himself wondering about that one. He hadn't seen a Shakamak Park Ranger tootling around on a golf cart in years, but that's about all the road appeared built for.

Other than the sound of their feet, everything about Shakamak was hold-your-breath silent. Yellowing vegetation formed a canopy overhead and enormous, oblong, podlike spiderwebs dangled at eye level. To one side of the path was an outhouse and on the opposite side was an old gazebo with a picnic table below it. They passed a worn metal barbecue grill mounted in cement.

Mark threw and spun the football, playing catch with himself.

They could see the water now. Lenape wasn't the biggest lake in the park—Lake Kickapoo was—but it was by far the most impressive. With clean, blue-green water and nice, grassy shores all around, it was perfect for fishing, camping, or just hanging out. Lily pads the size of CDs lined the water's edge at the end of the road.

"You throw my ball into the water, and you're going in after it," Casey warned.

Mark stopped next to a sign that read "Largemouth Bass Protected Length Range: 12-15 Inches." He drilled the ball at Casey. "I'll catch, then." He took off running along the shore.

Neal took the cue and ran after.

Casey smiled inside.

"Woohoo," Mark shouted as Neal chased him. "That's what I'm talkin' 'bout."

Casey dropped back, eluding imaginary defenders. "Craver's got Field Jordan beat! Wood goes deep!"

The pass bricked off Mark's hands and rocketed into the water, skipping several feet out from shore.

Without hesitation, Mark high-kneed it into the lake, pretending he was still running his pass pattern. Water splashed all around him; he resembled a crazy dog barreling in for a swim on a hot summer afternoon.

Casey and Neal both laughed.

Mark cupped his palms and dipped them into the lake. With great theatrical flair, he brought up two fistfuls of water and splashed them against his forehead. He slicked his hair back and shouted, "Come on in boys! The water is *fine*."

Casey shook his head and chuckled.

Neal mumbled something that might have rhymed with "black bass."

Mark snatched the football off a wave and chucked it toward shore. The ball landed in the lily pads directly in front of Neal with a splat.

"So," Eric said casually, "what's the problem with your car back there?"

"Lost my keys."

Eric turned toward Kevin. "Bummer."

They pulled up to the Jasonville Motel.

"Thanks for the ride."

"No problem, sir."

Kevin got out, but did not close the door. "Hey, let me ask you a question here, *Eric*. I mean, man-to-man."

"Yeah?"

"What color paintball mask do you own?

The charm went away in an instant. "*What?*"

"You know, *colors*—like red, black, white. Which one do you wear?"

"I don't know what you're talking about."

"Okay, glad we cleared that up." Kevin took a step away from the truck toward the motel. "Hey, thanks for finding where I needed to go without even asking. You must know your way around Jasonville very well."

Eric reached over and closed the passenger door with a slam, then peeled out of the motel lot.

AFTER A GOOD NINETY MINUTES OF TOSSING THE BALL AROUND and chillin', the boys piled into the car. Casey drove back the long way through the park, around the other lakes. He felt pretty good about things, confident that they'd lifted Neal's spirits.

They came to a clearing in between Lake Kickapoo and Lake Shakamak and Neal suddenly yelled, "Stop!"

Casey stopped, and Neal got out. Mark shrugged and stayed in his seat.

Neal stood with his arms crossed, staring into the forest.

Casey walked over toward him. "What's going on?"

Neal did not reply.

"Neal?"

Again, no response. Neal wiped his eye.

"C'mon, man, talk to me," Casey said. "What is it?"

"I just...in this spot." Neal took a few steps, like he'd decided to walk away, then stopped.

Casey glanced toward the car and saw Mark watching but not getting out. "What about this spot?"

"Trisha and I, we'd come here and watch the stars at night. On top of my Camaro...we'd...*oh God, I loved her!*" Neal went down to one knee and began yelling partial sentences. Borderline hysterical. Painful stuff to hear. "Never loved any...nobody else. How could this have hap—? Why didn't I stay? Why? A few minutes longer. All she needed! My life...*ours*...mine...over forever!"

Casey didn't know what to do. He put his hand on Neal's shoulder.

Neal continued, "Man, I miss her. I *can't* take it. No! I don't think I can live with—"

Mark came up and whispered in Casey's ear: "Dude, I've got to go now."

It was two hours since Kevin had been dropped off at the motel. His body ached worse than anytime since he'd been stung by a jellyfish in his early twenties.

He sat down on his bed and groaned, but he could take the pain level now. Earlier, he hadn't been so sure how he was going to manage. The tough part was trying to figure out what to do next.

Should he go to the police? Leave town before something even worse happened to him? Pick up a baseball bat at Shakamak Sports and go searching for Eric and his buddies? Retire from journalism and join a monastery?

Best immediate option: Buy aspirin.

He'd also need to get on the phone about his keys. Maybe Carlson or O'Malley could get into his apartment and FedEx him the spare. There must be a locksmith in town. Or he could search the friggin' cornfield.

No thanks.

There was always the coat hanger trick. Did that work on newer cars? Kevin glanced at the closet. Problem was, he'd never learned how to hotwire.

In a way, he understood. The car was distracting him from the business at hand, and harsh reality began to sink in. He stared at the welts on his face in the mirror across from his bed. There was no going back, no opting out at this point without regretting it until the end of his days.

Something very twisted was going on in Jasonville, and he needed to do something about it. He wasn't a cop. And he wasn't the greatest at eluding three guys in a cornfield. But there was something he could do. The one thing he knew how to do best: *write*.

He gave himself forty-eight hours to find answers on his own. Then he would either go to the police or head back to Indy.

Someone banged on his door. He grimaced and staggered over to the window. It was growing dark outside. He couldn't tell who was at the door. Apparently peepholes hadn't yet made it to small-town Indiana motels.

"Yeah? Who is it?"

"It's…Ja…fr…the…nt…dsk." The words were garbled but he could tell it was a female voice. Kevin opened the door.

Ms. Pro-Choice-On-Motel-Smoking stood outside his room. She held a set of keys in her hand.

"Someone left these at the front desk. With a note that said they might be yours."

"Really?" He took the keys, which were indeed his. Every key was in place. "Thank you."

She took in his appearance. Kevin had one horrific welt on his face and was walking with a bit of a limp.

"You all right, son?"

"I'm fine. Really enjoying my stay in Jasonville."

She gestured toward his face. "Get into it with someone at the bar?"

"No, it's nothing. I'll be fine. Just a bump or two, ma'am."

"Okay then." She nodded and turned away.

CASEY SHOT AN INCREDULOUS GLANCE TOWARD MARK. "WHAT? Hey, now's not the time."

Neal noticed. He stopped sobbing and rose.

"Guys, man, I'm sorry," Mark stammered. "I wasn't going to say anything. But I'm already late and *need* to get home. Like ten minutes ago."

"Mark, I said not n—"

"No, that's fine," Neal cut in, and started toward the car. "I gotta get out of this place too—like *now*."

"You sure?"

"Yeah." Neal opened the door. "Drop me off at my car on the way." He got in and waved his hands toward the steering wheel. "Just drive."

twenty-three

KEVIN COULDN'T GET HIMSELF TO SETTLE DOWN FOR THE NIGHT. He'd fall asleep for short spans and see images of paintball masks menacing him. He glanced at the clock and groaned when he saw it was 1:00 A.M.

He also kept worrying about his new car, and rationalizing that since they'd brought back his keys, they obviously wanted him to get it and leave town.

Okay, maybe not obviously.

He got an idea and decided to take action. Even though it was dark out and he knew walking was probably the only option at this hour, he got up and threw on some clothes.

The truth was, he *needed* the story and *wanted* his car. And he was used to living from one risk to another, until one finally killed him. He knew that a nighttime walk through the town could also be important for investigative reasons.

Kevin guessed the journey would take him about an hour, maybe more. Jasonville was only a few miles from one end to the next, and the motel was in the middle. Whoever had turned in his keys obviously had access to his car, if he—or they—had wanted it. Would it even still be there? Kevin headed out.

He walked along and paused when he came to the intersection of Sycamore and Meridian Street. He was only a few blocks from where Cameron Ford had been hit by Police Chief Rix's cruiser. He studied the dark streets and neighborhoods.

How many people had been out and about on the Friday that became an unspeakable night of carnage and terror? What had they seen, felt, heard?

He continued walking. Beth Simmons, age sixteen; Geena Wolford, Claire Borden, and Trisha Geller, all seventeen; and Karen Vothman, age eighteen. Had they felt toyed with that night before they were killed, as he'd felt in the cornfield?

At the intersection of Ridge Road and Possum Hollow he spotted a police car that had pulled someone over. The red and blue flashing lights lit up the dark neighborhood.

He tried to get closer to whatever was going down without being noticeably nosy. It didn't seem too serious; a fortyish woman being written up for a traffic offense.

Kevin didn't really want to go to the cops about his car and the attack in the cornfield. Not yet. If someone ever conducted a psychological profile on him, it would probably show he had a death wish.

But he'd been threatened before. Once during the Butler mess he'd come home and found blood—not human, presumably—smeared on his door. In this age of the internet, people seemed to know everything. Even as an investigative reporter with an unlisted number, always keeping key sources anonymous, some people still found a way to target him. He'd learned a few things about how the game worked.

His mind kept returning to one overriding principle as he made his way through the Jasonville night: Innocent people don't play mind games. They don't have the energy or the motivation.

So here in Jasonville, Cameron Ford sat behind bars, but someone was really trying to make Kevin's life miserable. Wasn't liking his presence.

Why would that be?

He was almost to the northeast edge of town.

Jasonville Water Works stood at the putative end of the city limits. It had a big parking lot that was lit up like a ballpark. The church was another half mile or so up the road. Kevin checked behind him, and saw no one.

He stopped in front of the green "Jasonville" highway sign he'd passed earlier in the day. The sign didn't list the population or anything, just the name of the town. A smaller, white sign attached to the lower left post advertised the "Crimestoppers" tip line, with a message assuring callers of cash rewards and total anonymity, and featuring a handcuff where the "O" in "stoppers" should be.

How did a town of 2,500 in America's heartland get to this point? Kevin shook his head.

In the distance he could now make out the Tiburon, still parked where he'd left it. Trying to hurry, but being careful at the same time, he jogged up to the car and checked the tires. No slashes. *Good.* He unlocked the driver side door.

He scanned the parking lot before getting into the driver's seat.

Have fun asshole.

Everything was silent. Kevin was only feet away from the cornfield.

He took a deep breath of the night air. A red paintball mask suddenly appeared from the rows and Kevin flinched.

No.

He blinked, looked again, and saw nothing.

You're losing it, Gibson.

He got in and closed the door.

Kevin saw a note. This time it wasn't his imagination. Someone had taped a note on his gear shift.

WE KNOW WHO YOU ARE.
NO ONE WANTS YOU HERE.

LEAVE…

OR YOU'LL ENJOY OUR NEXT MEETING EVEN LESS.

Kevin set the note aside and turned the ignition. Glancing in the rearview mirror he saw a bright pink splatter. Kevin spun and stared across the road opposite the cornfield. Nothing but trees. He looked more closely, and saw that the splatter was on the inside of the glass.

He gritted his teeth, shifted the car into drive, and hit the brights. He circled the lot, letting the Tiburon's halogens pan the field in front of him. Nothing.

"Unreal."

Kevin drove toward the motel. He rubbed at his face and pulled his hair back, checking the rearview mirror, ignoring the paint. He was still figuring out Jasonville's language, but he knew someone—Eric maybe?—had just told him where to go.

But the rules were changing. *He* was going to change them. And before it was over, he'd make sure they understood *his* language.

NEAL JORDAN'S CAMARO SCREAMED AROUND A CURVE. Music pounded relentlessly, at ear-splitting level. He didn't care. He shifted gears and tossed his last empty bottle of Bud into the backseat with the other five.

Faster.

He turned the music up and accelerated. His subwoofer pounded. Another curve was coming up.

Why care?

Guitars wailed through his speakers.

Trisha...

Nearly *decapitated* is what they'd told him. How? How could *anyone* possibly—

The car slid for an instant but recovered.

Why care!

"You'll find someone else someday," his mother had told him. Meaningless words from someone who didn't believe them, who couldn't possibly know if they were true.

She didn't understand. *No one* understood, not even his

so-called friends. Trisha had *always* understood him. She would understand now, too, if he could somehow see her again.

You'll find someone else someday.

Neal shook his head.

Screw someday.

Sometimes he'd wondered what it would be like to give in to the voice. Finally, for once, give in to the voice.

Give in.

In front of him were trees. The road ahead curved left. He could turn the wheel and follow the road—the road to more life without Trisha—or he could just not follow it anymore. He wanted to be with her, in whatever place she was right now, more than anything.

End it!

He floored the gas and gripped the wheel, holding it steady as the pavement began to curve.

Trisha…

He unbuckled his seat belt; dug his fingernails into the wheel.

The Camaro crossed over the median and went off the road.

"Trisha!"

Then careened straight into the trees.

twenty-four

KEVIN HAD ALWAYS BELIEVED THAT MINIMAL DISTRACTIONS were the key to writing greatness. The writer's zone, where everything flowed as easily as a Hawaiian stream, had eluded him for longer than he cared to admit. Fortunately, his Jasonville motel room was more distraction-free than his cubicle back in Indianapolis.

He sensed a temptation he had experienced before: that *this* story was *the one* that could make his career, with opportunities—and possible financial windfall—to follow. He didn't want to allow questionable motives to influence him this time. Kevin remembered a younger version of himself and his shallow fantasies: *The New York Times, USA Today*, O'Reilly, Larry King, the British media, maybe Australia—big exposure and big bucks.

As he typed an e-mail on his laptop, he began not to care as much about accolades and bank accounts. The welts on his face were a motive all on their own. The cornfield experience had taught him something; he'd tasted dirt there in more ways than one. The story of the Jasonville murders could potentially be more important than his Butler exposé. And, as best he could tell, no one else was going to write it.

For the first time in his life he felt motivation coming from a different place. Like the truth alone might actually matter most. It was an oddly freeing perspective.

He might not be able to make the earth shake, but he was

gunning for something along similar fault lines. He would need to move quickly.

Kevin fired off the e-mail to the *Tribune*, thankful his motel room came equipped with optional internet in addition to ashtrays. He closed his Macbook and mulled Draft One, Part One—an investigative article that would be the first to raise questions about a lone killer being responsible for the Jasonville carnage. He didn't quite have enough to make it fly...yet. There were some pieces still missing, but he thought he might know where to look.

LORRAINE WASN'T SURE HOW TO BROACH THE SUBJECT WITH CHIEF Rix. They'd just gotten back from the site of a horrible car crash east of town. People were still using the term *accident*, rather than a certain *other* word. Studying the face of Bertrand Rix she knew that he, too, was wondering how long that would hold.

Rix was one of those men who always just seemed *in charge*. He carried himself with a humble swagger, no matter the circumstance. Lorraine wasn't romantically attracted to him, just impressed with his ability to lead whenever things got tough. She marveled at the seemingly bottomless reservoir of masculine confidence he possessed. At the same time, she wondered: How could it possibly be endless? What kind of chaos would envelop them if Rix's reservoir ever went dry?

She took a deep breath and relayed the latest bad news, "Cross just called to say he has the paperwork ready to file five counts of murder against Cameron Ford, first thing tomorrow morning. He said he didn't need to talk to you. Just wanted to give you a heads-up."

There was a pause. Rix made a face at her like he had an oversized tarantula on his desk. Then he exploded from his chair and cursed. Before Lorraine knew what had happened, Rix's pen was ricocheting off the opposite wall. A Greene County map rattled loudly and came to a rest.

Lorraine waited to see if there would be more.

Chief Rix sat back down in his chair. His desk was cluttered, and he looked like a man who hadn't slept or shaved in the past forty-eight hours.

Lorraine closed the door and walked over and picked up the pen. She pulled up a chair across from Rix. "So…"

"Yeah?"

"You've got me wondering about something, Chief."

Rix did not reply.

"Let's talk about why that bothers you so much."

Half an hour later, Andrew O'Malley was on the phone with Kevin.

"There's definitely a story here," Kevin told his boss. "And it's going to jar some people."

"Controversy?" O'Malley asked.

"Hard to say."

"What about sensational?"

"Undoubtedly," said Kevin.

"More there than just Cameron Ford?"

"Without question."

"That's what I like to hear," said O'Malley. "Send us the first part in the next twenty-four hours, and we'll run it on page one this week."

"Done."

"Oh, and Gibson?"

"Yeah?"

"Watch your back."

"I will."

O'Malley's assistant was trying to tell him something, but he didn't miss a beat. "I'm serious this time."

"Yeah," Kevin said, "I got it."

"Well, for starters, deep down I don't really believe Cameron Ford was trying to kill me in the graveyard," declared Rix with enough cold sobriety to make a Memorial Day checkpoint proud.

Lorraine tried not to blink. "Okay."

"Ask me 'why not?'"

"Why not?"

"Because when he had the chance, his attack was tentative. When I had the advantage, he was dangerous. But when *he* had it, he didn't take me out."

"Maybe he had some sort of problem with doing a cop, but no qualms about killing high school girls. A psychological barrier."

"Maybe. But he couldn't quite manage to kill the Redmond girl either."

"She's lucky to be alive. Actually, you both are."

Rix leaned forward. "I'm not convinced."

"Well, what's it gonna take to convince you?" Lorraine replied.

"Hope Redmond was more petite than any of the other victims. Why could he succeed with them but not with someone even more vulnerable?"

"There's no accounting for toughness, sir," said Lorraine. "Or will to live. Or dumb luck. Any of the above."

Rix turned in his chair. "Did I ever tell you about the Bradford case, four years before I landed here?"

"Nah."

"It was a trial a colleague of mine testified in. This Bradford guy killed his wife. And not simply after some domestic dispute. It was something he'd planned for months. Very distasteful. He shot her in cold blood with a stolen gun. People swore he was at work that day. He almost pulled off a perfect crime. But as the guy got into his car after the murder, he made eye contact with his next-door neighbor. Bradford could've just shot the neighbor, but he disregarded him. The neighbor proved to be the only eyewitness between him and freedom."

"Okay, you've lost me."

"Sometimes there's only one genuine witness standing

between truth and travesty." Rix tapped his pen. "This has never happened before, but I think *I* am that witness."

Casey's mom and dad sat at the kitchen table. She drank tea while he read the newspaper. Their son was upstairs listening to music, probably surfing the internet.

"Do you ever worry that we might have made a mistake leaving First Community?" Shirley Wood asked her husband.

Duane Wood stared back. "No. I mean…what does that have to do with anything?"

She wasn't buying that and tried to let him know with a look.

"C'mon, dear," Duane said, "do you know how many people have left churches over the years and their communities weren't rocked by murders?"

"Well, Casey—"

"—didn't have anything to do with it. He *saved* a girl."

"But he started hanging out with Cameron Ford and those other boys right after we left."

"That doesn't change the facts. And it didn't *cause* any of this. I know it's been tough. We knew these kids and their parents. I feel for the families, this community, as much as anyone. But don't start up with that."

"Haven't you wondered even a little if—"

"No."

"Okay." She sipped from her cup.

"Our son's a good kid," Duane said. "So he's been into some weird things lately. How uncommon is that during the teenage years?" Duane paused and studied the napkin holder. "We both know Casey, his morals. Give him some credit. He understands what lines not to cross."

"Still."

The phone rang.

Duane shot up. "I got it."

She listened to his firm "Hello," then put down her cup as his tone turn serious.

Duane hung up the phone.

"That was Neal Jordan's mother."

"Yes?"

"Neal..."

"What?"

"...was found dead this morning."

She set her teacup down and it made an abrupt clanging sound. "What? How?"

"He wrecked his car into a tree."

"An accident? That's terrible."

"No."

"What do you mean, *no*?"

"They're saying it looks like he committed suicide."

"So what would you be testifying to, if you're called as a witness?" Lorraine asked Rix.

"That Cameron Ford didn't kill anyone. He tried to, but something in him—tentativeness for whatever reason—kept him from succeeding."

"So who killed all those girls?"

"That's the million-dollar question, and one our fine County Prosecutor doesn't give a flip about."

"Okay, what's the answer? We have the wrong guy in jail? I mean, he still stabbed you."

"What if it wasn't just one person?"

"What? Where did that idea come from?"

"My imagining how this case might go if I hadn't been stabbed."

"Lucky you."

"Yeah, lucky me. Remember this, Lorraine. Whenever a case seems easy, ask yourself what your assumptions would be if the biggest clue *hadn't* fallen into your lap. Lots of cops like to skip this part. I think it's just a form of laziness masquerading as efficiency."

Rix's phone rang, but he ignored it.

"Incidentally, what did you find out about Friday the thirteenth?"

"The films or the day?"

"I already know about the movies. What about the day?"

"Friday the thirteenth, historically unlucky."

"Why's it unlucky?"

"Well, for starters Friday's the day Jesus died. And the number thirteen thing goes back to Norse mythology."

"Norse mythology? I might need a refresher."

"Okay." Lorraine flipped open her notepad. "As the story goes, an evil god, Loki, crashed a party in Valhalla that was meant for only twelve people. In the process, he caused the death of the god of joy and reconciliation."

"That's terrible."

"Yes."

"I don't think I ever learned that in school."

"Sorry, Chief," said Lorraine.

"So score one for bad history in Norse mythology. But this business about Jesus dying on a Friday...I thought that was good." Rix rested his pen on his chin and started tapping it.

"Come again?"

"You know, 'Good Friday.'" Rix spoke and tapped. "How did that end up in the bad luck column?"

"No clue," Lorraine said.

"So basically we have an unlucky day established by a bunch of drunk Norwegians, plus Christians who apparently don't understand their own theology."

"Right, Chief."

Rix stopped tapping. "So where does that leave us with Cameron Ford? Cross wants to introduce the movies as a motive. I don't think it will fly with a jury. But he's been known to throw in everything but the kitchen sink into his cases."

"I'm sure the obsession with the movies will have an

impact," Lorraine said, "but it's not going to match up all nice and tidy."

"No kidding," Rix snorted.

"Okay…so let's assume your gut is right on this. How do we make it right?"

Rix tossed the transcript of the Tommie Moorer interview over toward his deputy. "Actually, when I said that I was that one witness, that might not be totally right. There might be another."

Casey's parents called him down from his room.

And they were staring back at him *way* too seriously.

"What is it?"

His dad spoke. "Son, Neal Jordan's mom just called. His car was found crashed into a tree."

"He crashed his Camaro?"

"Yes."

"That sucks. Is he okay?"

His dad looked down at the floor. "He didn't make it."

"Huh?"

"He's dead, Casey."

"Wh…what did you say, Dad?"

"That your friend is dead. I'm so sorry, son."

But I was just with him.

"No."

"Oh, honey," said Casey's mom.

"How? Mark and I were just with him yesterday."

"There was nothing more you could have done," Casey's dad said. "Apparently, he was too messed up over what happened to Trisha. Worse than anyone realized."

"What are you saying? How did he—"

"Honey," his mom said, "Neal crashed his car intentionally."

Casey stared across the room at his mom's china. "No!"

"Son," his dad said, "we're so sorry."

Casey collapsed back onto a chair. "I can handle this."

"Oh, baby," his mom said.

"I can handle..." he said again, but his voice didn't sound right.

Neal just killed himself.

Casey couldn't make eye contact with either of his parents. He looked at his mom's china again, then at the baker's rack next to it. There was the breadmaker they'd gotten his mother for Christmas, collecting dust. He clenched his jaw, then held his face in his hands. He looked slowly up at his father.

"Dad, no. It *can't.* I..."

His hands started to shake.

Casey's mom and dad glanced at each other.

He broke down into violent sobs and fell to the floor.

"Not *Neal!*" he screamed.

Casey pounded his fists on the floor. His mom was crying. His dad was trying to pull him up.

"OH GOD, *NO!*"

twenty-five

"WHY WOULD THEY TREAT THE MOORER KID LIKE THIS?" Lorraine said. "Isn't he like twelve?"

"Turn to the page I highlighted," Rix replied. "Gets even better."

She flipped ahead and read. "So the kid's mom brings him in. We're slammed, so we let IBI cover it. Then they end up probably scarring him for life."

"I hope that's not the last word on it," said Rix, "but yeah."

"So why did they treat him like a hardened criminal?"

"His last name has some history associated with it. An older brother who has told lots of lies to law enforcement—confessions that were bogus, names dropped that led nowhere. Let's just say the system isn't fond of him."

"So these IBI guys found out and tried to nip that in the bud," said Lorraine.

"Here we are," Rix went on, "big important case, prosecutor wants swift justice, they think we have our man. Then comes forth this concerned mom dragging her kid in, claiming he saw something suspicious the night of the murders. He refuses to ID Cameron Ford, despite ample goading from law enforcement. Something doesn't quite add up with the presumed scenario. The problem witness happens to be the kid brother of a known liar."

"And Agents Zane and Jergens weren't buying it. They didn't want to bite."

"Right," said Rix, holding up his finger. "But it's not that simple. They know that if the kid doesn't point them to Ford again, then the case has a hole. These guys don't like being called to the stand by defense attorneys who needle them with the 'Did you look into other possible suspects?' angle *ad nauseam*. Everyone hates it. I hate it. Cross…don't even get me started. But here's the thing: Once in awhile, there's something to it."

Lorraine smiled. "So you think he saw more than he's telling, for whatever reason."

"Now you're tracking with me, Deputy."

"And he didn't want to give it up because he's still scared of something. And their prickliness didn't help."

"Prickly?" Rix's eyes widened. "That's pretty close to the word I would use."

"Got it," Lorraine said. "So do you want me to ask Tommie about what he saw that night? Maybe try the nice cop routine and not drag his brother's name back through the mud?"

"No." Rix rose from his desk. "No," he pointed his thumbs in toward his chest. "*I'll* ask him."

"Okay."

"But you *can* do me a favor in the meantime."

"Yes?"

"Take another look at the Geller crime scene." Rix slid on his coat. "I want our department to conduct a second search of the area. You know, fresh eyes and all that."

Casey sat on the edge of his bed, staring blankly around the room, swallowing the rage that surged whenever his eyes fell on the picture of Neal, Mark and him as kids.

Crows squawked outside his windows.

Neal.

Casey's mind drifted. He was in the passenger seat of Neal's Camaro, three months ago.

The two of them had been driving, jamming out

to a modern rock station on Neal's new satellite radio, a birthday gift from his parents. Suddenly, Neal whipped the car over to the side and killed the music. The next instant, he was out of the car. Casey could see something black in the middle of the road.

A single crow hobbled along, unable to fly. Neal ran toward it, just as an old green truck with rusted-out fenders appeared.

The truck swerved *toward* the bird and went right over it. Neal stopped dead in his tracks. Casey watched helplessly.

The wake of air from the moving vehicle knocked the crow over and sent it spinning, though the tires and undercarriage missed. The truck's driver and his buddy yukked it up, proud of themselves, glancing at the rearview mirror and laughing.

"Did you see that?" Neal said without looking at Casey. "They knew I was trying to—"

The truck sped away. Neal ran over to the side of the street and picked up a rock.

"Bastards!" he yelled. Neal uncorked a ferocious throw. The rock sailed through the air and nailed the back of the truck, right inside the middle "D" in "Dodge."

The truck didn't stop. In fact, Casey noticed, the brake lights never even came on.

At Neal's behest, Casey held the weakened bird in the passenger seat while Neal drove. They went to the vet's office, but it was closed.

Neither of them could figure out what was wrong with the crow. No broken wing or anything. It just wouldn't fly. Somewhat reluctantly, Neal and Casey released the bird in a field just outside of town.

They drove to Trisha's house. Neal didn't say a word about the crow. When Casey made a comment about the two Neanderthals in the truck, Trisha started asking questions.

Neal didn't try to play up his role. As Casey told the story, Trisha's expression changed, and she gazed at her boyfriend a little differently than before. Suddenly Casey felt like a third wheel.

He remembered thinking he'd never had a girl stare at him that way. He wondered if he ever would. Casey ended up leaving them alone and walking home that day.

A crow cawed outside his window.

Neal and Trisha were both gone.

Casey's gaze went from the window to his *Freddy vs. Jason* movie poster. He stood, face to face with the poster.

Winner Kills All.

He scowled at the images.

The mask. The blades.

He thought about the Order. About Neal. And Cameron.

Casey ripped the poster off the wall and tore it in two. Then he picked up the pieces and tore some more. And tore. And tore.

"And why would I let her talk to you?" Guy Redmond demanded. "Even if she was feeling up to it."

Kevin and Guy stood in the hallway at the hospital, Guy effectively blocking Kevin's path.

"Mr. Redmond, please understand. If—and only if— she feels up to it, I would appreciate any consideration." Kevin unfolded a newspaper article and handed it to Hope Redmond's dad, along with a business card.

A CNA walked by and eyed them curiously.

Guy glanced at the article's headline, a holdover from Kevin's past success:

BUTLER VICTIM'S PARENTS PRAISE
LOCAL INVESTIGATIVE REPORTER

He scanned the first few paragraphs, then looked back at Kevin, still wary.

"Look, I'm not about to help your daughter's attacker

get off the hook or confuse the investigation," Kevin said. "I'm trying to steer the authorities in the right direction, just like I've done before. Respectfully, Mr. Redmond, *something is wrong here*. I just have a few very simple questions about what your daughter saw.

"If I'm wrong...well then, Cameron Ford is still in jail. If I'm right, then someone else who may have been involved in what happened to your daughter and those other girls may still be out there."

Guy's expression softened just a bit.

"I want to help you and the other parents of Jasonville," Kevin said firmly. "But you have to help me help you."

The phone rang, and when his mom said it was for him, Casey guessed it was either Jeremiah or Mark. He didn't feel like talking to either of them, but he took the phone anyway.

"Hello?"

"Casey?" It was Ashley Tyler, and she sounded upset.

He skipped past the greeting. "Did you...hear about Neal?"

"No. What about him?"

"He killed himself. Drove his car into a tree."

There was silence on the line.

Finally she whispered, "That's horrible."

"Look, it's not really a very good time right now for me to talk. I'll call you later."

"No, I need to..."

"What, Ashley?"

"...tell you something," she said, her voice shaky. "I realize the timing is awful. I..."

"What is it that can't wait?"

"I think I missed my period."

twenty-six

LORRAINE STEPPED OUT OF THE CRUISER AND SURVEYED THE Geller residence: a lovely mist-blue, two-story house with a gorgeous three-panel picture window facing the street. The yard was immaculately maintained, with rose bushes and dwarf pines in front of the relatively new home.

It also happened to be a homicide scene. So much for the assurances of safety she'd given her mother back in the day.

She walked to the front door and took out the key Rix had given her.

Mr. and Mrs. Geller and their son were grieving with family in South Bend. By the looks of the stain that was still visible on the front porch, the family might never be back.

Hard to blame them.

Lorraine unlocked the door. She stepped over the stain, into the home, and said a silent prayer.

Her eyes went from the stain, to the Geller's couch, and that's when she realized something didn't seem quite right. Her instincts were trying to tell her...

Behind you.

She whipped around.

A car drove by. The sound of its engine faded and all was quiet.

Nobody appeared to be watching. Life was as sleepily small-town normal as could be. That is, if one could somehow forget that a teenage girl had been murdered in her doorway.

Lorraine closed the door. She got her bearings and proceeded through the house, taking notes.

The living room had been left exactly the way it was the night Trisha was slain. Except the sofa and a La-Z-Boy recliner were now in their correct spots. Lorraine panned the room and recalled the contents of the police report. A smoked glass coffee table sat in the middle of the living room, with an aspen wood candle on top. She wondered when the family had left the house. Perhaps within days.

The back door was new, but some splintering was still visible near where the doorknob met the frame. The killer had breached the home in no less than three places, possibly four.

Lorraine headed upstairs. She tried to envision Cameron Ford being here. Pursuing. Not relenting. She gazed at the pictures on the walls. One of them showed a curly-haired boy in a black T-shirt holding up a turtle. Another was of the family on a beach, waves crashing in the background. She stopped before a vacant spot in the collection. A light outline of where the frame had been mounted was still visible. The nail still hung in the wall. She thought about the cracked frame they'd collected. Another clue that provided no direct connection to Cameron Ford, or anyone else.

She headed to the bathroom. The screen on the window had not yet been replaced. She knew they'd confiscated the ladder the killer had used. She went into the master bedroom and stopped in front of the television, which, for some unknown reason, had been on at full volume when Trisha Geller's body was discovered.

She picked up the remote and hit the power button, then stepped out in the hall, cranking up the volume as she backed away. Some talking head on a news program blathered on about the price of oil. She tried to think.

Strange.

Lorraine turned off the TV and went to Trisha's room.

She'd seen stuff on the news about parents who lose kids in tragic ways, how they sometimes can't get themselves to clean out the bedroom. As if keeping the room unchanged preserves some shred of life. She hoped Mr. and Mrs. Geller didn't end up that way long term.

Trisha's room was a tribute to the typical teenage girl—an adolescent heading toward full womanhood while holding on to a remnant of the child. A pink comforter covered the bed. A Green Day poster hung on the wall above the headboard. A worn pair of jeans, a shirt, and a pair of socks lay crumpled on the floor.

Trisha Geller's murder was unique for several reasons. The killer had been in the house a long time, which demonstrated a lot of determination, but had left behind very little evidence. And not one shred of physical evidence pointed to Cameron Ford.

Which meant what?

Lorraine stared at a shelf that had a crystal unicorn and some books on it.

Which meant it was hard to believe that Cameron Ford had been here, unless he just lucked out by not leaving any evidence behind, then got careless as the night went on.

She thought about the little girl who had probably grown up in this house, in this room. A young lady who'd sat on this bed and daydreamed about life.

Then she pictured that night. In horror films, the killer never stops coming. Trisha Geller had been in a real-life horror movie.

Lorraine imagined it all again, and a chill ran through her veins.

Maybe he did leave something damning behind, something they'd just missed before?

She walked slowly out of Trisha's room and down the stairs.

BLOOD WAS ON BERTRAND RIX'S MIND AS HE WAITED FOR A callback from Mrs. Velma Moorer. Problem was, he wasn't sure who it belonged to.

Two blood types had been found at the Geller crime scene. One belonged to the victim. The second to the killer. Presumably.

Then again, it might belong to another family member. Or some other individual with no connection to the case. One person it *didn't* belong to: Cameron Ford.

In fact, Cameron Ford's blood wasn't found at *any* of the murder scenes. He'd voluntarily given a sample, saying he hadn't killed anyone, then declined to say anything more. He'd shown no signs of injury, other than the bruises he received from his collision with Rix's car. Hope Redmond's blood was type O negative. A slam-dunk blood pattern rare enough it wasn't mistakable for anything else. His own blood was type AB. And Cameron Ford, a confirmed B.

No other blood types were present on Cameron's clothing except Rix's own and Miss Redmond's. Had Cameron Ford somehow cleaned up before the final murder? Could he have had time? The homicides were all bloody— Trisha Geller's particularly so. Cross would never agree, but forensically the case was a mess because there wasn't more of a mess.

Had Cameron Ford somehow known he was going to get clipped by a police car and leave behind only traces of Hope's blood type?

Unlikely.

There *had* to be something more going on here. Rix realized he'd been squirming in his chair. He couldn't wait to interview Tommie Moorer.

LORRAINE MADE HER WAY TO THE GARAGE.

When Trisha Geller was found, the garage door was up. A neighbor said it was closed when he'd left that Friday for his shift at a convenience store in Terre Haute. According to the neighbor's estimate of his departure time, it would have been not long before Trisha's 911 call.

Why did that matter?

She studied the pattern of the stains on the floor. There was sawdust scattered across one section of the garage, not collected because it had no bearing on the case. Not stained, presumably.

The scenario had bothered Rix, and she was beginning to see why, seeing it up close.

Speaking of seeing things more closely.

Lorraine noticed a piece of jagged metal poking out from under a utility shelf, barely visible. Could they have missed something important here before?

She moved closer and crouched down. She slid the item out. A saw. With a brown stain on it.

Lorraine winced. Could be nothing. Could be huge. She would take it back with her.

To cover all the bases, she hit the garage door button. Up it went, loudly.

The noise rattled on. Another disturbing image popped into her head. From a horror movie. *Scream* maybe? A garage door used as a murder weapon. She shuddered.

She scanned the street, shooting a glance toward her car. Her eyes popped open.

A masked kid, staring right at her.

He stood with fists clenched, forearms partially extended. Like a bodybuilder flexing, preening.

Goading her.

Nodding.

Taunting.

She got a good look at him. "You!" She pointed.

He ducked down behind her cruiser. She set the saw down on a workbench and raced across the street.

She stopped at her car. Had he gone right or left?

Everything was sickeningly quiet.

Then, a shed in the yard to her right rattled. She rushed over and found a large rock at the base of the shed. The little prick had thrown it against the metal siding to distract her.

She realized she'd left the Geller crime scene unprotected. The garage door was still up, the entrance to the house unlocked. The saw was out in the open. She headed back, and decided it was time to call Rix.

Somehow the masked kid had gotten across the street. He was now to the left of the Geller house, in between the garage and the neighbor to the south. He flipped her off.

"Hey!"

He gave her the bird with both hands, then took off and hopped over the fence.

"Stop!"

Over the fence, like it wasn't even there.

"I said *stop!*" She ran.

She got to the fence. Dogs barked, seemingly from several directions. A rug fluttered on the neighbor's clothesline. Her hand drifted to her firearm.

She wanted to pursue, but had no idea which way he'd ran. The cold reality was the masked kid had managed to give her the slip. Lorraine reached for her handheld to radio Rix and thought about how she was going to word what she was going to say.

Her mind raced through the facts as she knew them: Trisha Geller had been murdered here. Cameron Ford was in jail awaiting trial, his black paintball mask locked away in a vault, marked as people's evidence. And somebody wanted to intimidate her...or else had a very brazen, sick sense of humor.

twenty-seven

KEVIN PARKED OUTSIDE THE RESIDENCE OF MS. ANNA VATHENS, mother to one Eric Vathens, a name he'd found next to a photo from a Jasonville High yearbook.

There were no cars in the driveway and the garage door was closed. He saw no sign of Eric's black Toyota truck. Kevin didn't picture Eric as the park-your-vehicle-in-the-garage type.

Nothing struck him in particular about the neighborhood. Pretty quiet, middle class, nothing in too bad of shape, nothing standing out as different.

A police car drove past.

He'd done some research and discovered that Eric didn't have a dad. Or at least one in town.

What did he expect to find?

First: He was curious how much the kid's mom might talk about the Jasonville murders, and where her dear son was that night. Second: He wondered if there might be a picture of Eric—maybe in the living room or on the fridge, if the latter was visible to the casual visitor—that might show him and/or his friends in all their paintball-playing glory. He still wanted to know the answer to the question he'd posed to Eric.

What color mask do you own?

Which young cornfield terrorist were you?

And was that the extent of your involvement?

Third and lastly, Kevin wanted to run into the kid again. As he raised his hand to knock on the door he didn't think it was likely that this was the day. But he'd be seeing him again, one way or another.

Three knocks later, no one answered. Kevin peeked into the living room window. He heard a noise and drew back.

Footsteps, urgent ones, approaching the door from inside the house.

The door opened a crack. A weathered-faced woman with brown hair gazed sheepishly back. "Hello?"

"Are you Anna Vathens?"

"Yes, may I help you?"

Kevin opted for the truth. "My name is Kevin Gibson, from Indianapolis; I'm a journalist with the *Tribune*." He handed her a business card.

She took the card, looked it over. "What are you doing on my doorstep, Mr. Gibson?" she said, handing the card back to him.

"No, please, that's yours to keep." He nudged her hand. "And please call me Kevin. My paper is covering the Jasonville tragedy."

"What happened to your face?"

"Oh, it's nothing. Is it true that your son, Eric, was close friends with Cameron Ford?"

"*No*. And you didn't answer my question about your face."

Kevin grimaced. *Your son happened to my face.* "I'm sorry, what was your question again?"

"Never mind, Mr. Gibson—"

"*Kevin*. Please call me Kevin."

"I'm sorry I can't be of help. Eric and Cameron went to the same high school. That's all I can say. Twenty-five hundred people live in Jasonville. Of course they knew each other. That's it."

"You're sure?"

"May I ask why Eric's friends matter to your newspaper?"

"Well, the police are still investigating, as is the *Tribune*."

"What does that have to do with Eric?"

"Maybe nothing."

"Maybe?"

"The people of Indiana want to know the full story. Jasonville is big news. And not only statewide, the entire nation wants to know more. My paper just doesn't want to miss anything."

"I don't know what more I can add." She exhaled stale graham cracker breath in Kevin's direction.

"Is Eric around?"

"No, he isn't right now, as a matter of fact."

"Out playing paintball, perhaps?"

Anna Vathens stared at Kevin. "Why are you really here, Mr. Gibson?"

"As I said, I'm investigating th—"

"To smear my son and his friends?"

"Your son and his friends? Now you're putting words in my mouth, Ms. Vathens. No, I—"

She stepped back, putting her hand on the doorknob.

Time for a recovery attempt. Kevin tried to sound soothing. "I'm sorry, help me understand…which friends are we talking about here?"

"Cameron Ford had lots of friends besides Eric. Talk to their moms."

"Really? Who?"

"No, stop. Hold on." She took a half-step back. "I can't really get involved."

"Just tell me their names, and I'm off your doorstep and onto theirs."

"Why are you so eager? What are you after?"

"Friends' names. That's all."

"You didn't have to come here to find out those. Why start with Eric?"

"Okay, I'll be more specific. Eric's paintball-playing buddies. Those are the friends I'm most interested in."

"I never said Eric played paintball."

"So you're saying he didn't?"

A pause. "No, I never saw anything…"

Anna Vathens's voice trailed off. Her carotid artery appeared to quiver on the right side of her neck.

Ah yes, one of his favorite physical tics. Often exhibited by the unpracticed liar.

Kevin tried to sound casual. "But we both know better, don't we, Ms. Vathens?"

"What?"

"Your son—he owns a red paintball mask. He's been seen around Jasonville wearing it."

Again, Ms. Vathens did not reply.

"Surely, being his mother, you know—"

"That's enough." She drew back again, ready to close the door. Then she stopped. "No wait, I think I get it." She pointed at Kevin's face. "Is this why you're all worried about who plays paintball 'round here?"

Something didn't feel right in Kevin's chest. He thought he saw a hint of a smile come across the face of his interview subject. He locked his jaw and stared hard. The woman's eyes now seemed…not right. She might be a bit mental. Or maybe she was just wistful. Then the look morphed, and he thought he saw something else. Regret, maybe? Or fear?

"Can't help you," she mumbled.

"I just need some answers, Ms. Vathens. It seems you might have a few. Why won't you share?"

"Hasn't this town been through enough?"

"As a mom, you'd do anything to protect your son. Wouldn't you?"

"My son is a good kid. You tell your big city newspaper boys to keep his name out of it."

"A red paintball mask: yes or no?"

"I'm telling you, Eric is a good kid."

"And now *you're* not answering *my* question."

"Yes. That's the one part you've got right." She slammed the door shut before Kevin could get in another word.

KEVIN WAITED OUTSIDE THE HOUSE, THEN WATCHED AS ANNA Vathens' car disappeared up the street.

Ding-dong, the witch is dead...

He fixed his gaze on the house and pondered the ethics of what he was about to do.

There weren't any.

Or, at least, nothing good he could come up with other than The Story was king, and he had to submit to it. If that meant breaking and entering, violating laws, trampling on rights and ethics, then so be it. He'd always found it was better to break laws before going to the police with the unearthed dirt, rather than after. All about managing rapport.

He'd haggled with Hope Redmond's father at the hospital, but in the end her dad had decided the girl was too weak to talk. Now getting stonewalled by Mama Vathens had put him in the mood to get some answers his own way. He was sure she was covering for her son.

He slipped out of the car and crept over to the side of the house, over the fence, and into the backyard.

Kevin had kept his eyes and ears peeled for any evidence of dog ownership the first time around, when the lady of the house had slammed the door in his face. Hence, jumping into the backyard wasn't that big of a gamble. Just illegal.

He tried the back door and found it locked, which he'd guessed was about a fifty-fifty proposition in Jasonville, Indiana. Maybe the percentages had changed since the murders. He worked the lock.

Back in his college days, he and his fraternity brothers used to carry out for sport what normal people called "breaking and entering." And they did it for the most collegiate of reasons: food. One night, Kevin snuck into some yuppie two-story house and raided the freezer. He made off with four Cornish hens—a haul that his frat brothers had found hilarious for some reason. He wouldn't have guessed at the time that he was in training for moments like this.

He jimmied the door loose and stepped inside.

Hi honey, I'm home.

He heard nothing.

He inhaled a scent like a combination of laundry detergent and cat litter.

The plan was to check for pictures on the fridge and anywhere else around the house, keeping his eyes open for anything odd, then find the kid's room. And be quick about it.

If Eric Vathens was the red-masked cornfield assailant, fine. One strike. If he'd been involved in more than that, then all the better.

The house wasn't one of Jasonville's finest. It looked like only mom and son lived there, but that was enough. The sink was full of dishes, and there were various items of clothing and empty cereal boxes lying around pretty much wherever. The carpet needed a serious cleaning. A lamp in the living room had been left on. Kevin thought it best to leave it that way.

The upstairs revealed little, other than that mom slept on an old-school waterbed. Kevin headed downstairs to the basement, and soon found what had to be Eric's room.

It was everything Kevin had expected, except no paintball mask. No paintball anything, in fact.

The walls of the room were graced with pictures of porn, interspersed with various horror movie posters. Eric had tons of DVDs from every horror movie franchise imaginable: *Friday the 13th*, *Texas Chainsaw*, *Halloween*, *Nightmare on Elm Street*, *Psycho*, *Child's Play*, *Evil Dead*, *Scream*, and on and on. Some Kevin had heard of, some he hadn't…and was glad.

Where would a teenage boy stash his paintball stuff? Somewhere other than his own bedroom?

Kevin beheld the mess. What would be the point of hiding something elsewhere, when the kid could obviously have left just about anything he wanted sitting out in the open? Mom didn't seem to mind. She probably never came down here.

He stepped over to the TV/DVD combo system and thumbed through a stack of movies that looked like recent rentals. There was a pair of DVDs from the *Faces of Death* collection, "shockumentaries" from the eighties that Kevin knew were supposedly actual footage of real death scenes shot around the world. The director later admitted faking much of the nastiest footage, but the videos remained popular among teenage boys. Another DVD was called *Paradise Lost*, and from the look of it the film had nothing to do with the John Milton classic. Kevin popped open the case.

Empty.

He hit the power button on the TV. When the DVD menu came up, Kevin made his selection.

Ominous music and a collage of disturbing images filled the screen. This *Paradise Lost* was a documentary feature about a grisly triple murder in Arkansas, the victims elementary school boys. The introduction explained that police arrested three local teens who were tried and convicted. Railroaded, some people claimed.

Kevin stared at the TV screen. He knew he should keep his visit brief, but found himself intrigued.

Images of the young victims, all second-graders—eight-year-olds—flashed across the screen. Then came crime scene close-ups. Kevin cringed.

An odd sound came from the TV—or was it the TV? He stopped the DVD and was sure about what he'd heard.

He was no longer alone in the house.

Footsteps.

Hurried.

Frenzied.

Kevin froze and listened.

The noise was too chaotic to be Mama Vathens. The classic entrance of a teenage boy.

The sound increased as someone descended the stairs.

Kevin reviewed his options and they all sucked. He slipped into the closet and closed the door as quietly as possible.

Eric came into his bedroom and tossed something on the bed.

Kevin tried not to breathe. He was standing among piles of clothes, shoes, and a few dirty towels—trying to hide and not succeeding very well. If Eric opened the closet door, Kevin was toast. But there was nowhere else to go.

Things got quiet. Kevin listened but he couldn't tell where Eric was.

A cough rang out from just outside the closet door, and a chill shot up Kevin's spine.

He tried to scrunch back further against the back wall of the closet.

A long minute passed.

Too calm and quiet.

Kevin made a fist and prepared for the worst. His mind raced through various scenarios, none of which he liked, none of which got him out of this insane position he'd gotten himself into.

Still too quiet. Was Eric still in his room?

The telephone rang. Kevin tried to calm the resulting jolt of panic that ripped through his body.

Eric answered and began to speak as he wandered around the basement. Kevin exhaled and tried to listen.

"No, no." His voice came from another room. "Not gonna be a problem."

"No, man, that's not going to happen."

Kevin was irritated that the kid's voice kept fading in and out, but what was he going to do, complain?

"Yeah, man, but first I gotta take a sh—"

Kevin heard a few more words, but couldn't make them out. Then a beep.

He waited.

A loud sliding sound. Then, water.

He waited a minute to be sure.

The shower. *Yes.* Eric was taking a shower.

Kevin gave the kid another minute to get all nice and lathered up; maybe have soap in his eyes, water in his ears.

He eased the closet door open. As he lurched out, his shoe caught on something buried in the back of the closet.

A sock-covered foot.

Huh?

There was something there, buried among the piles of clothing and shoes. Kevin reached down. It was soft. He saw a pant leg. He pulled and saw a pair of women's jeans.

Eric had a stuffed pair of jeans, resembling a female lower body, stashed in his closet.

In another setting, maybe harmless...

Kevin hesitated, not liking any of the thoughts and possibilities that came to mind.

The water was still running in the downstairs bathroom. He took a final glance around the room and bolted.

HE WAS OUT. *FINALLY* OUT. HE RAN.

He hurried toward his car while his mind raced.

Is Eric Vathens a killer?

Kevin reached the car and peeled out.

Or a normal teenage boy?

He checked his rearview mirror.

Who could tell the difference?

Kevin was a well-paid, highly trained investigator and even he couldn't answer with certainty. And that fact disturbed him, almost as much as the question.

twenty-eight

CASEY STEPPED OUT OF THE CAR AND TOOK IN THE BEAUTY OF Shakamak State Park and Lake Lenape at dusk. He needed some peace and a place to think.

Clouds were forming across the skyline; darkness would be coming soon. He saw lightning in the distance. Whether it was coming toward the lake or moving away, and how quickly the storm might be moving, he couldn't tell.

He didn't care if he got struck by lightning. He felt like he already had been.

On the drive out, he couldn't help himself. He'd driven by the spot where he, Neal, and Mark had been four days before.

He still didn't want to believe it.

The sun dropped down slowly to Lenape's forested horizon. The water sparkled with the last flickers of light. He stared out across the lake and thought about Ashley. She'd spoken very little to him the past few days at school.

He felt the hair on the back of his neck stand up and his skin crawl. He heard thunder, closer now. Casey held his arm up to his face, level with his eyes, and saw goose bumps. He'd left his coat at home.

Casey saw a fisherman in the distance—up the bank and around the curve of the lake to the southeast. The guy was working the water with persistent casts, probably trying to land one last bass before the storm.

The rain held off for now, so Casey decided to walk along the grassy, yellow-green shore.

As a kid, he'd always liked coming here and exploring the nature trails. Once he'd gotten his driver's license, this had been his favorite spot to come whenever something was bothering him, his personal place of retreat that no one else knew about. Sometimes he tried to talk to God. He would stare at the ripples on the surface of the lake. Waiting.

There was never any reply written in the water, and Casey had wondered why it couldn't just be that simple. He decided one day that maybe the man upstairs had already written an answer of sorts, but he'd written it *with* the water.

It all seemed like so long ago, a different version of himself. So distant.

The sky turned darker and the wind picked up ever so slightly. The storm was moving closer.

Casey knew his mom and dad wouldn't want him to be out here under these conditions. He looked back toward his car.

They also wouldn't want to be grandparents just yet.

The twilight sky lit up with lightning, and the thunder cracked close enough to make Casey flinch.

The fisherman kept fishing, though, and Casey figured he was probably safer than the guy and his graphite pole.

But why, really, should he care about his own safety? Beth Simmons, Karen Gothman, Geena Wolford, Claire Borden, and Trisha Geller had been murdered. All girls he and his friends had talked about. Neal hadn't been able to take it...and was...*gone*. Cameron was in jail. The Order was in shambles.

He thought of Hope often, still in the hospital, still having problems, and it just made him sick.

And he wasn't even sure that was the worst part.

How was he supposed to even contemplate fatherhood right now?

He waited for another bolt to light the sky, one that might take him out of his misery, but none came.

Two minutes passed before another flash appeared. It

wasn't even close. Part of him knew he could never go the way Neal had gone; that he would never do anything that willingly short-circuited his future; that the days to come might be better.

If he lived that long. *If* his parents didn't kill him. If something in Jasonville didn't kill him before.

He felt numb. He took a deep breath and took in the smell of impending rain. The air seemed eerily electric.

The wind wove its way through the trees, then the whooshing sound faded into the sound of the water lapping onto the shoreline.

Casey heard a loud, frantic shout.

He glanced up at the fisherman.

"Hey-hey!" came the cry.

The fisherman had been working his way toward Casey. They were a lot closer to each other than he'd realized.

"Yo, check it out!" The fisherman laughed like a little kid.

Then Casey saw what it was about. The fishing pole was bent dramatically, and the guy was battling hard against a monster catch. Casey's eyes widened and he hustled toward the clearing where the fisherman struggled.

"Some of the best fishin' when it's stormy, my friend!" the man shouted with raucous enthusiasm. He widened his stance and jerked the pole back and forth.

Casey strained to see the line. It was already too dark to see very far out without a flashlight.

"Dude, my reel gave me this huge cast…was way out there…oh, I've got him. I've got…hoo man, this boy's gonna be huge!"

Casey saw the fisherman's line in the water, zigzagging crazily. The pole's tip was dancing all over the place. "Don't let him break the line," Casey said.

"Yeah, buddy, come to daddy! He's tiring. He's tiring."

A lightning strike shredded the nighttime sky, and Casey thought it must have hit one of the trees along Lenape's shore to the east.

The fisherman was stunned. "No!"

The fish was taking the line toward a patch of downed branches about fifteen yards from shore.

"Stay outta there!" Casey yelled.

"No way!" the fisherman cried. He cocked his body the opposite direction.

"Don't let it get off," Casey coached. "Don't...!"

The line disappeared into the branches, and the fisherman's reel made a wrenching, snagged sound.

"No!" the fisherman pulled and jerked, but that just made it worse.

"Careful," Casey said.

"I can't believe...no, he's gotta still be hooked!"

"Careful."

"Gotta get it out, man."

"Easy, now."

"Okay, okay, I'm gonna give it some slack." The fisherman held the line tight, then popped the cast button on his reel and whipped the pole toward the snag.

Still stuck.

He tried again, with the same result.

Casey could tell the guy was getting frustrated. "Hey, maybe try—"

The fisherman popped the reel again, then twice more, each try more frustrated than the last. He waded out into the water, pulling more line out of the reel with his fingers, giving the snag a ridiculous amount of slack. He reeled in a little, then jerked wildly.

Something snapped loose, but the fisherman's violent tug sent lure and line flying high up into the air and to the left, where it got snagged in a partially submerged tree.

"Oh...perfect!" The guy was on the verge of a total meltdown. Casey felt sorry for him.

There were now two snags: one in the tree and the one in the water where the hook was, presumably no longer with the fish on the end.

Feeling there was nothing he could do, Casey turned to leave.

"No, wait. I can still feel somethin'. Somethin' *big* still on the line, man!"

The fisherman kept at it, and somehow made progress. Casey could see the line coming up out of the water, with whatever the hook was currently snagged on in tow. He saw something long—that wasn't moving and didn't look very fishlike—mired in a glob of moss and branches.

"What is that?"

The guy waded in and handed Casey the pole. "Just reel slowly. I'm gonna go out there farther and see if he's still hooked."

Casey did as he was told, though he knew the part of the line that was wrapped around the branch wasn't coming loose at any point in this lifetime. It would soon be too dark to see anything, and the storm clouds weren't looking any friendlier. "If the fish got loose, maybe just cut the line."

"Just hold 'er steady a minute. He's gotta be in there." The fisherman pulled a small flashlight from his pocket.

"No, dude. I saw the lure come out."

The fisherman ignored Casey's comment.

The water was getting choppy and waves jostled the snagged mass. Casey reeled in the line a bit, and some of the moss and other lake guck fell off and splashed into the water.

"Hey, what'd you do?"

Casey could see something long and thin dangling from the line. He felt a raindrop on his head, then another.

The fisherman sloshed toward shore in a hurry. "Give me that."

He took the pole and reeled, bringing the object higher above the water.

"I don't think that's your fish," said Casey.

"Yeah, I'm thinking you're right," the fisherman replied, almost in a whisper.

More raindrops came.

Thunder.

"Well look at that," the fisherman said.

"What is it?"

"A spear," replied the fisherman.

"What?"

"For spearfishing. Underwater."

"Huh?"

"Yeah, guys go down there, like scuba, but to fish. Someone must have lost it. But I didn't think that kind of fishing was legal here."

Casey couldn't see perfectly, but the fisherman's hook appeared to be lodged on the shank at the tip of the spear.

A smashing crack of lightning came, illuminating the clearing. It was so loud and bright that the fisherman dropped the flashlight.

Casey wondered how long it would take to get back to the car. He'd had enough excitement.

"Check that out!" the fisherman pointed toward the spear.

The rain picked up, and the lake came alive as drops of water pelted the surface.

Casey wasn't sure if his eyes were seeing right, but the tip of the spear seemed to glow bluish-white, a flamelike haze shooting up toward the clouds.

He felt an uncomfortable tingling sensation in his fingers and toes.

"Hey, I'll bet lightning's about to strike here," the fisherman declared.

The spear glowed like a roman candle. A real-life St. Elmo's Fire. Casey's uncle used to tell him about how the horns of cattle would glow in a bad thunderstorm. Casey had never seen anything like it before. "Cut the line," he said.

"Look at that, man, that's crazy."

Casey didn't want them to attract the next monstrous lightning bolt that was surely coming. "Cut the line, *now!*" he repeated.

The fisherman obliged.

Gradually the spear slipped down and disappeared beneath Lenape's surface.

Casey wiped rain from his face. And then it hit him, something he'd heard on the news.

Geena Wolford had been impaled with a spear.

"Fish maroons me and I come up with *that*," the defeated fisherman said, and threw his pole down. "Man, I've had it with this place!"

A spear that hadn't been recovered.

Another lightning flash hit on the other side of the lake, and the fisherman started to collect his gear.

"Hey, that's too bad about your fish," Casey managed to say. "You gonna be all right?"

"I'm never fishin' here again!"

"You need a ride?"

"No, man," the fisherman said. "My truck's over there." He pointed north.

"Sorry about the fish, man. You had him."

Rain started to pour.

In fact, none of the weapons Cameron had used had been recovered, except for the knife he stabbed the cop with.

"He cheated!" the fisherman shouted.

"Right," Casey replied. "He cheated." Then he ran toward his car.

Back in the car, Casey remembered that a sighting of a St. Elmo's Fire was often said to be a favorable sign.

But he didn't feel good about it at the moment. Maybe it had something to do with him almost getting fried by lightning.

He cranked his wiper blades full blast and pulled out.

Casey had never seen that spear before, but he thought he might know someone who had.

When he saw Mark again, he'd have to ask if he was right.

twenty-nine

LORRAINE WAS SITTING UP FRONT BEHIND THE COUNTER Thursday night when a young man wearing a black hoodie sweatshirt came in through the door.

And promptly asked to see Cameron Ford.

"Your name?"

He hesitated a moment. "Mick."

Lorraine nodded toward the entrance. "A little late to be coming by for a visit, isn't it?"

The young man did not respond. He also wouldn't look her in the eye.

"What's your last name, son?"

Another pause.

She decided to play along. "I can tell him you're here…but we need a last name."

"Donald."

Lorraine stood. *What was this?* "Your name is Mick…Donald?" She tried to keep a straight face.

"Yeah."

"What's your relationship to our inmate, Mr. Donald?"

"He's my friend," the young man replied, fidgeting. "My *good* friend."

"I'll check our list," she said nonchalantly.

"List?"

"Yeah, it has family, friends, lawyers, spiritual advisers— you know, everyone's names. So we know who to expect."

"Oh. Then I'm probably not on it."

"I thought you said you were good friends?"

"Look ma'am, I just wanna see Cameron Ford a minute."

"Shall I ask him if he wants to see you...Mr. Mick Donald?"

"No." The kid's voice got quieter.

Lorraine noticed he was playing with something in his pocket.

She shifted her body so he could see her cuffs, then her gun. "Young man, I'm going to have to ask you to take your hands out of your sweatshirt."

He complied without hesitation, and she could tell he didn't have anything. She realized she'd been a bit on edge ever since the masked figure at the Geller residence.

"Are you going to let me see Cameron or not?"

"No."

"There isn't a list, is there?"

"No."

"So you lied to me," he declared.

Lorraine rolled her eyes. "What's your real name, son?"

"Brandon."

"Brandon *what*?"

"Wolford."

The last name registered in her mind as the same as one of the dead girls. Lorraine grimaced. She tried to speak calmly, "You know what, Brandon...I didn't recognize your face when you came through the door. That's a good thing. Let's keep it that way."

"What're you saying?"

"You didn't really come here to *visit* Cameron Ford, now did you?"

He paused. "No."

"What do you think this stunt is going to accomplish?"

"I don't know," Brandon replied. "Don't really care."

"Sure you do."

He shrugged. "You the only one here?"

"Chief Rix is in the conference room on a call," Lorraine

lied. "Officer Hayes is back watching the monitors." In reality, Hayes was probably watching TV, but that might not sound quite as good.

"Oh."

"May I give you some advice, Brandon?"

"What?"

"Leave and don't come back."

Silence. Then: "You don't understand."

"I'm sorry about your sister—more than you can even imagine. But trying to deal with things this way is going to hurt your family even worse in the long run."

"I loved my sister. And Neal Jordan and I played football together. He was a good guy. And Geena…" His voice started to crack. "Geena was special. You don't know how—"

"And *you* don't know how close you are to landing in a cell of your own."

"I just wanna know why."

"Leave now, Brandon. Turn around. Walk out. And I'll pretend this never happened."

He stood still for a moment, as if what she'd said left a loophole somewhere.

Finally, he left.

Lorraine let out a breath.

She went in search of Hayes.

It appeared he'd gone home for the night without bothering to let her know.

Slacker.

Lorraine went back to the front counter.

Twenty minutes later, Brandon Wolford returned.

With two friends.

Brandon's eyes were wild this time. One of the friends held a baseball bat. They all looked ready to go.

"What's going on boys?" Lorraine said, as casually as possible, though she activated a button under the counter.

"We wanna see the chief."

"Why?"

"Because," Brandon said, "he ain't here now."

The trio started toward her.

"Don't try to come any closer," she replied, and drew her gun.

The one with the bat sneered, but they all stopped.

Brandon said, "You gonna shoot all three of us?"

His question was a good one, and she wasn't entirely sure how to answer. "No. Because you and your pals are going to turn around and leave."

"You'd shoot us to protect a murderer like Cameron Ford?"

"I can't let you assault or kill a defenseless inmate."

"We don't want to hurt you. We just want him."

"Not gonna happen."

"Think lady," Brandon said. "You can just tell them we got past you."

"Because no matter how many bullets you fire, one of us *is* going to get past you," Bat Boy added.

Lorraine pointed her gun at Bat Boy. "Well I just made up my mind, and it's for sure not going to be *you*."

Bat Boy's cocksure grin went away.

"And I'm guessing none of you has any idea what a bullet feels like when it pierces your skin and rips through muscle and bone," Lorraine added. "Not a pleasant thing."

None of the boys said anything, but they held their ground.

"Hayes," Lorraine yelled toward the back, just to buy time and create some doubt in their minds. "Get up here!"

They laughed instead.

"We saw your comrade at Quick-Mart pumping gas ten minutes ago."

She shook her head.

"We know it's just you here…and *us*."

Bat Boy tapped the bat against his hand.

"It doesn't matter," Lorraine said. She tried to think ahead and didn't like any of the scenarios she envisioned.

Shooting up the station and three teenage boys was about the last thing she wanted. She was in over her head and knew it. She needed to buy time.

"You're scared." Brandon declared.

"And you're wading in so deep you're not going to get out."

"You think I care? He drove a spear through my sister's chest while she slept."

"Yeah, but you're not carrying out a lynching on my watch."

"He tried to stab your boss to death. You think he's gonna mind if we take care of the psycho?"

"Yes." Lorraine squeezed the pistol tighter. "I do." She noticed the friend who didn't have a bat slink back a little.

"How's it going to look if you shoot us over the killer of Jasonville?" Brandon said. "They'll run you out of town."

Lorraine thought about it and realized there was a chance he could be right. Why was she protecting Cameron Ford? The answer wasn't readily evident, a fact she found disturbing.

"No," she managed to respond.

"You won't shoot us."

"I will."

"I think you're bluffing."

"I'm not."

"Why you being so difficult, lady?"

"Because I'm a cop who enforces the law. And I can tell you, he'll pay for what he did."

"My point exactly. So why wait?"

"It doesn't work that way."

"We can *make* it work that way."

"Wrong."

Brandon came forward, almost seductively. "Deep down, you don't really care if we mess him up."

"Stop."

"Just say we got past you. I'll even admit to it."

"No."

"Think of him spearing my sister and stabbing your chief. Plus all the other horrible things he did that night. What if it was *your* sister?"

"I told you to stop."

"You're going to let us in."

She felt sweat on her forehead. "Let me say it real slow so all three of you get it. Not...going...to happen."

Everyone stood still.

Someone approached the front door.

A middle-aged man waltzed into the station dressed in jeans and a windbreaker, wearing a ball cap, head down.

"Oh, sorry," he mumbled as he walked past Brandon and his friends.

The three vigilantes didn't know what to do. An awkward moment of silence prevailed.

Brandon stepped aside, gestured toward the counter, and said, "You go ahead, pops."

"Thanks."

The man made his way past the boys, then spun without warning, instantly coming face-to-face with Bat Boy. With amazing force and speed that betrayed his age, he grabbed the bat and slammed the young man against the wall, then lurched violently to the left, ripped the bat away, and spun around to face the others.

Lorraine thought about firing a warning shot, but didn't need to.

"Boys," Chief Rix began, "I can't tell you how much I hate having to come down to my station in the middle of the night for an emergency call." He turned to Lorraine. "What's the story here?"

"They think they're here to see Cameron Ford," she explained, "with a bat and an attitude."

Rix sized up the trio.

"Any laws been broken tonight, Deputy?"

Lorraine stepped out from behind the counter. "Not yet, no."

"Okay, then. Go home *now*. All of you. Pray and thank your God in heaven you didn't assault someone tonight. And that your chief of police is feeling forgiving."

Brandon locked eyes with Lorraine, and she saw a smile appear in the corner of his mouth. He nodded his head toward her softly, like he knew when he'd been beat.

"*Now!*" Chief Rix boomed.

Brandon and his buddies ran out.

The front door eased to a close. Lorraine returned her gun to its holster.

"Nice timing, Chief," she said.

"My pleasure. Where is Hayes?"

"Gone home."

"Perfect." Chief Rix pulled his hat up. "I gotta call the state patrol and tell them not to send anyone."

"Right. Hey...thanks, by the way."

"Oh, yeah, sure," he replied. "Call me anytime."

Lorraine asked, "How did you?" she paused and glanced toward the wall. "What about your shoulder? I thought you were injured."

"Oh, it burns like hell," he replied, then pointed the bat toward the door, "but *they* didn't know that."

thirty

Rain came down and dampened the streets in the Jasonville night. A shadowy figure stood outside the home of the late Beth Simmons and checked the time.

This was the place where it all had started.

He waited silently, gazing toward the front door of the house that was now occupied by empty nesters Dennis and Charlene Simmons. He guessed they probably didn't want to talk to him.

Beth's body had been found by her mother. The Missus had later suffered a breakdown and been placed on a mental health hold by the authorities, with the reluctant blessing of her husband. It was pretty common knowledge around town.

Apparently, she was out now, and they were back together. Though daughterless.

He lingered another moment, trying to relive the events of that night. He checked the time again.

Get moving.

The downpour continued as he made his way across town. He marveled at how unharried and nearly uninhabited the streets of Jasonville appeared. It wasn't like the storm was *that* bad.

He stopped in front of another house.

On the front porch, an ornately carved wooden sign

greeted visitors: "Welcome to the Wolfords," in bright orange letters.

Welcome indeed.

Unlike any of the other victims, Geena had been killed while her parents were home, her father and step-mother asleep upstairs—a particularly heinous and brazen murder.

He wondered if the Wolfords now slept with all of their doors locked.

A porch light came on. He held still and reviewed his inventory of rehearsed lines.

Nobody came out. False alarm. Probably just a motion detector.

He checked the time and headed north.

The amount of time it took him to get to the late Claire Borden's house bothered him a little. His recreation could turn out to be a challenge.

This time he stood a good, safe distance away from the porch. One, because he didn't want to excite any more porch lights. Two, because Claire's murder hadn't taken place inside the home.

She'd been found outside, near her car, the door still open. A discharged vial of pepper spray was found nearby. Claire's killer had had an ax.

The ax had won.

He found the spot where.

Even after two weeks had passed, and even in the rain-soaked moonlight, it was obvious. Near the curb in front of the Borden house the remnants of a stain were still visible, which he found both fascinating and disturbing.

He stared. He couldn't help it.

The house looked vacant, though there was no sign indicating the home might be up for sale. Claire's parents might have an easier time selling their house than some of the other families, though they probably would never see things in that sort of light.

He glanced around one last time.

Time's up.

KAREN GOTHMAN'S BODY HAD BEEN FOUND IN THE MIDDLE OF the sidewalk, near a friend's house.

He arrived at the scene a smidge out of breath. Again, it took him slightly longer to get to the location than he'd expected. He was running behind schedule.

From the sidewalk, he stared toward the house.

A friend and classmate of Karen's, Meghan Reed, lived there with her parents and younger sister. Karen had just left Meghan's house when she was murdered. She had not made it far.

A car drove by and sloshed watery slop into the gutter near where he stood. The driver paid him no attention, which was probably best.

Karen, like most of the other victims, had been attacked with a sharp instrument near her face and neck. She never stood a chance.

Or maybe her only chance had been to not come walking out of her friend's house that night, at that particular moment.

He took in the neighborhood and noticed the ample bushes to the left of the house. *Yes, many, many places to hide.* But there would be no hiding tonight. Only reliving.

He let it all soak in a minute, then hurried away.

THE HOME FORMERLY OCCUPIED BY TRISHA GELLER WAS VACANT and dark. A note from a family friend was posted on the front door thanking well-wishers and stating the Gellers would be back in a few days.

The murder scene at the Geller home was regarded as

having been the most grisly. Unlike the others, neighbors reported hearing commotion and screams. None of them responded in time, though.

Nearly beheaded in her own front doorway, Trisha Geller's body had been discovered by a neighbor. Her killer—Cameron Ford, if one accepted the police theory about her death—hadn't even bothered to close the door to conceal his crime.

Why would he take the chance of having her found more quickly?

The rain had stopped. He noticed that for a house under watch, no one appeared to be too troubled by his presence. But he had that covered, if need be.

He knew he needed to give this place more time. He didn't know how much, but he knew that getting to his next spot within a reasonable time frame was going to be next to impossible.

He checked the clock on his cell phone once more, then set out anyway.

As he arrived, harsh reality became crystallized. The problem with the final locale—the intersection at which Hope Redmond had been attacked—was that it was too far away.

Too far from either the Geller residence or the sidewalk where Karen Gothman had been found.

Too far for the timeline put forth in the charges filed against Cameron Ford to make any sense.

Still, he stood on the curb by the stoplight and studied the surroundings. Nothing stood out.

A few yards ahead, he could see a row of bushes near a small park. He guessed they were the ones where Hope Redmond hid from her attacker.

Hid for her life. Effectively, it turned out.

Score one for Miss Redmond.

He stepped out in the street and dared the stoplight to

reveal something. He watched it change from yellow to red, with no consequences. On such a night as this, the light seemed unnecessary. Why had the good folks of Jasonville even bothered?

That was one of the least significant of his questions.

Why try to stab someone at an intersection?

Houses...specific houses—no, *girls'* houses—had been associated with all the other attacks. Yet here was poor Hope Redmond, simply driving home, parked at a stoplight. A masked killer jumps in her car and tries to stab her to death. *Why?*

It was the one attack on a young woman that night that came off as truly arbitrary, if an observer went by logistics alone. Not only arbitrary, but misguided. The attack's lack of success seemed to verify that.

He looked out into the neighborhood and wondered if anyone relevant lived nearby. What detail was he missing?

According to her family, there was no known enmity between Cameron Ford and Hope Redmond.

So what had happened?

He heard a car coming—no, a truck. He got out of the way, out of the street, and watched the vehicle pass. Some old man in a cowboy hat, heading west.

Yes, this was a bad place to attempt a murder. Not to mention to cap a murder spree. Perhaps the killer was getting more and more bold as he went along? Kind of a Jack-the-Ripper-type thing?

Maybe. But he doubted it.

Too far away.

Not logical.

Another rub was that Hope Redmond, the final young woman attacked, had *survived*, and had been able to give the police a time before her body went into shock from blood loss. There was less margin of error with her testimony because it was the testimony of a live person. Live people were good witnesses. Murdered people had to rely on a coroner's estimate.

It seemed physically improbable, if not impossible, for one individual to have pulled all of this off.

That could only mean one thing...

Kevin Gibson replayed the timeline in his mind. He ran through various scenarios, even shaving some minutes off his journey here and there. He still couldn't make it fit.

As a writer, he didn't have to be sure about everything. Reasonable doubt was the domain of courts of law and juries. Actually, the right seasoning of doubt in a story made it all the more enticing to readers.

But he was sure about something.

The case against Cameron Ford had some serious, serious holes in it.

Kevin planned on filling in some of them. And he was pretty sure he knew with what...starting with an extra pair of jeans, at the right place and the right time.

thirty-one

TIFFANY MUELLER NOW WORKED AS A WAITRESS AT BECKY'S Haute Downtown Diner. Before long, she hoped she'd have enough money saved up to go back to nursing school.

"Can you believe what that guy in Jasonville did?" said Sarah Erbert, her coworker. "He's kinda cute, though, but in that sick, Scott Peterson sorta way."

Tiffany set an empty plate down and stared at Sarah, who was holding a copy of the *Indianapolis Tribune*. "Let's not talk about that."

"Oh come on! Don't you want to know anything about one of the most shocking murder cases in Indiana history? One that happened half an hour from here?"

"No."

Sarah shook the newspaper's pages. "Aren't you the least bit curious?"

"Well, I…" Tiffany began, then she dropped a coffee mug.

Sarah hurried over and picked it up. The wages at Becky's may have been meager, but the dishes were strong as cement.

"Is something, like, bothering you?" Sarah asked.

"It's nothing. No…well…just an incident that happened while I was at Hoskins'."

"That sporting goods store?"

"Right."

"Well?"

"Well what?"

Sarah crossed her arms. "You gonna tell me about it?"

"Nah, it's probably nothing."

"Out with it."

She opened her mouth to speak, but nothing came. She checked around the diner to reaffirm what she already knew. Becky's wasn't busy at the moment.

The truth, Tiffany realized, was that she really *wasn't* the tough chick she'd once thought herself to be. Something hadn't been right with her since that night. She'd tried to ignore it, bury it, and that had almost worked. But eventually she had to admit to herself that the Jasonville story—the merciless killer in a paintball mask—wasn't going to go away.

Sarah stared at her. "Girl, what gives?"

Tiffany sighed and recounted the story: Seeing the guy wearing a paintball mask as she was finishing up her shift at Hoskins'; being frozen with fear; him coming to the counter to pay for the mask; his cold sneer and dark eyes.

She stopped talking and poured herself a glass of water. Her face was hot and something felt tight in her chest.

Sarah had a curious expression on her face—almost too curious. "You ever tell the police?"

"No."

"Ever tell your boss?"

"No."

"Why?"

"He probably would've acted like it was me overreacting. I mean, there'd been weirdoes in the store before, though not as creepy, and the manager never did a thing. He just blew me off whenever I'd say something. Hoskins' always erred on the side of the customer. The guy had actually paid for his merchandise. End of story. I just quit. It was easier. I never would have thought..."

"Ever tell anyone?"

"No."

Sarah looked incredulous. "You just kept it to yourself?"

"Yes."

Sarah groaned. "Don't get me wrong, girl, but somethin' ain't right with that."

"But I didn't know. I wasn't sure."

"When you heard about those girls being killed by some freak in a paintball mask right after that, didn't you *wonder*?"

"I didn't want it to be true. Ever since I heard about it on the news, I've had nightmares."

"You're lucky to be alive."

"I know!"

Why couldn't she just shut up?

Sarah held up the newspaper. On the front page was a mug shot. "This look like the guy?"

Tiffany frowned. "Actually, no it doesn't."

Sarah plopped the paper down on the table in front of Tiffany. "Ya sure? Maybe you should take a closer look."

Tiffany stared at the picture. No matter how closely she looked, it didn't change one key fact.

It wasn't the same person.

"This isn't the guy who came into the store. Guess that's another reason I didn't say anything. I told myself it wasn't related."

"Well," replied Sarah, "the reporter, that Kevin guy, says some people have doubts that only one kid was involved."

"Wh-what?"

"Yeah," said Sarah. She cocked her head. "Maybe you should think about that one for a minute."

Tiffany lined up a salt shaker next to its pepper counterpart and centered the Tabasco.

"In your heart," Sarah asked, "do you believe the guy who was in your store was involved in the Jasonville murders?"

Sarah had always had a knack for asking just the right question. Or the wrong one, depending on how a person viewed it.

"Yes," Tiffany replied.

"Then you've got to go to the police. *Tell* them what you've told me."

Tiffany glanced at the clock. "All right, I'll go to the police, if *you* take me."

The present mood on the streets of Jasonville was cordial, Kevin had discovered. Helpful? That was another story. No one had shot anything at him recently, which represented progress.

Though he received a few "no comment" replies as he asked questions, he usually gained some reasonably helpful, though anecdotal, information. He just needed a little more—what was the word—dirt?

No, not dirt.

Depth.

Kevin had always used different means to get his information, depending on the person. He could do firm, condescending, funny, therapeutic, creative, friendly, concerned, suggestive, colluding, scheming, conniving, or manipulative. Over the years, he had utilized each technique to varying degrees. He had his strengths as a journalist and investigator, but he liked to think versatility was the top one.

He hung out on a bench near the Quick-Mart, studying people as they went in and bought a newspaper or a Twinkie, or pumped gas. He did his best to strike up conversations without seeming too obvious.

A young man approached the store and entered. There was something intriguing about his stride, but Kevin's glimpse was too brief to draw a definitive conclusion. He kept his eyes on the Quick-Mart's entrance and waited.

Kevin visualized the task at hand as the journalistic equivalent of Tetris. Through experience and ample practice, he'd become a master at spinning the pieces so they fit right. There might be a gap somewhere, but he could always worry about filling it in later. That is, of course, as long as he got everything else lined up neatly.

The kid emerged. Kevin folded the newspaper he'd been pretending to read and stood. He walked straight ahead.

The young man headed directly toward Kevin, carrying an oversized soda. In his mid-to-late teens, he had short blond hair and a medium build. Just under six feet tall and pretty well dressed. He appeared to be about the right height and build.

Images flashed in Kevin's mind. A black paintball mask, beckoning him into a cornfield. A white Greedo, stepping into a row and cutting him off. Shooting. Pain. Then a blood-red mask, with cornstalk hair dripping down off the chin. Himself screaming. He blinked and the images were gone.

Kevin examined the kid more closely—the walk and mannerisms—and he couldn't quite put his finger on what was bothering him. The kid's eyes rose and met his. Kevin waited for some hint of recognition. Irritation, perhaps, that he was still in town? He didn't see any.

The young man said, "Whatup?"

Kevin stopped like they knew each other. "Hey bro, you live around here?"

"Yeah."

"Ya got a minute?"

"Uh, I guess so."

"My name is Kevin Gibson. I'm a reporter for the *Indianapolis Tribune*. Maybe you can help me."

"Why are you still in town? I thought most of you people had done your reports and cleared out."

"I'm here trying to understand more about you and your classmates."

"Is that right?"

"Yes, and—"

"Who do you want to know about?"

"I'm sorry." Kevin smiled and extended his hand. "As I said, it's *Kevin*...and your name is?"

"Jeremiah."

They shook hands.

"Jeremiah what?"

"Bronson."

Kevin made note of it. "Like Charles Bronson?"

"Who?"

"Never mind. Do you know what's been in the news lately about your town?"

Jeremiah took a sip of his soda. "What do you mean?"

Kevin patted the newspaper in his hand. "You aren't aware of what's been in the news?"

"Newspapers…news…oh right, what have I heard?" He cocked his head and eyed Kevin strangely. "Wait, no, I got it. Ford—that's the word. I hear Ford's been in some trouble."

"Ford…yes…clever. You're a funny guy, Mr. Bronson."

"Yeah, I'm hilarious to everyone. It's in lieu of character."

Kevin suppressed a smile. "I'll bet."

"You seem like you probably know what you need to know already," Jeremiah said with a shrug. "Don't see what more I can offer you, sir."

"Kevin."

"Right. Don't know what more I can tell you, *Kevin*. The story's been pretty much everywhere."

"Maybe you can tell me more about Cameron Ford."

Jeremiah was silent. "Not sure I should talk about that."

"How about some of the girls he killed?"

"They're dead, and I can't change it." He took another swig of his soda.

"Do you know a kid named Eric Vathens?"

"Maybe."

Kevin frowned. "What's that mean?"

"Used to hang out…with a group of guys that included him. Not so much anymore."

Interesting.

"What did you guys do together? Did Cameron ever hint at doing something like what the police allege he did?"

"I'm not supposed to talk about it," Jeremiah replied, and Kevin knew by his body language he was on the verge of losing him. He tried a different track.

"How well did you know those girls?"

"Well enough. Made me sick when I heard."

"What about Neal Jordan?" Kevin asked. "Did you know him well?"

"Neal was..." Jeremiah started coughing, choking on his drink. When his voice came back it had softened to a raspy whisper, "one of my best friends."

Kevin kept quiet a moment. "I'm very sorry."

"Please don't write anything bad."

A cell phone ring interrupted them with a polyphonic version of the Lone Ranger theme song. Jeremiah pulled the phone from his pocket, checked the number, and then mumbled, "Excuse me."

Kevin tried to listen in. Jeremiah's face betrayed little. He had no nervous tics. His eyes were brown and honest. Kevin couldn't ignore what his gut was telling him.

Not one of the paintball shooters.

His head, however, was insisting that there was something worthwhile to uncover here, if he kept at it.

Jeremiah was trying to act nonchalant, but the phone conversation was obviously difficult. He kept repeating "I will" and "okay" in a dry monotone. When he clicked the phone off, his demeanor was different. Less chipper.

"You okay?" Kevin asked.

Jeremiah hung his head and mumbled some words that were hard to hear above the noise of a diesel truck that was idling in the Quick-Mart parking lot. "Neal's parents" were all Kevin heard clearly. The truck revved its engine and pulled away.

Kevin weighed the moment. "Was that call about your friend, Neal?"

"Yes."

"He killed himself, didn't he?"

"Yes."

"Depressed over his girlfriend?"

"You know about that?" Jeremiah dropped his soda cup, spilling Coca-Cola and ice along the sidewalk.

"I do," Kevin replied and stepped back.

Jeremiah gazed down. "Didn't taste right, anyway."

Kevin kneeled and picked up the cup.

Jeremiah uttered a bland, "Thanks."

"You know…from what I hear, people seem to think Neal Jordan and Trisha Geller would've ended up at the altar someday."

"Probably. You gonna write about that?"

"I might."

"Put it in an article in your paper?"

"Possibly…unless someone convinces me otherwise."

"Don't say anything that would make us look bad."

"Who's 'us?'"

"Us…Jasonville…Neal's friends…and Cameron's."

"I'll do what I can," Kevin replied. "May I ask you for an honest opinion?"

"About?"

"The possibility Neal Jordan killed himself because it was going to come out that he was involved with Cameron Ford and the murders."

"No way. Anyone who told you that's full of it. No one who knew Neal would ever think that."

"Did Neal play paintball?"

"What?"

"Did Neal Jordan ever pl—"

"I heard you. No."

"How about you?"

Jeremiah flinched. "Don't go there."

"Why?"

"You're headed in the wrong direction."

"Then this is your chance to point me in the right direction."

"What if I don't want to?"

"I think you do. You care. I can see it in your eyes. That's why you're talking about it even though someone tried to tell you not to."

"But—"

"I like you, Jeremiah. So I'll tell you what I've got right now, and you can tell me where I've got it wrong."

Jeremiah turned and checked the Quick-Mart behind him. He turned back around. "Lay it on me."

Kevin put the newspaper in his back pocket. "Your former friend, Cameron Ford, embarked on a killing spree, for reasons known only to himself so far. He murdered four female classmates; Beth Simmons, Geena Wolford, Karen Gothman, and Trisha Geller. He also attempted to murder classmate Hope Redmond and Chief of Police Bertrand Rix. Trisha Geller was the girlfriend, and likely future fiancée, of your pal, Neal Jordan, who in the wake of everything tragically committed suicide. Some people have doubts Cameron could have acted alone. There are some time-line issues. Other people are convinced there's more to the story. Personally, I wonder if you have any buddies who might own paintball masks...and an unhealthy interest in murder."

Jeremiah was shaking his head.

"You're shaking your head at me."

"You're perceptive."

"Why are you shaking your head at me?"

"Maybe I shouldn't say."

"There more to it?" Kevin asked.

"Yeah...more," Jeremiah replied. "That's one way to put it."

"Okay, I'm listening."

A grimace.

Kevin waited.

Finally Jeremiah asked, "Didn't you say your name was Kevin?"

"Yes."

"Gibson, was it?"

"Correct."

Jeremiah cocked his head in recognition. "Wait a minute—*the* Kevin Gibson?"

"Last time I checked."

"The one who busted all those cheats up at Butler—who broke the story about those players, what they did to those girls?"

"Yes, I am precisely *that* Kevin Gibson."

"Dude, my dad's a huge Hoosier fan," Jeremiah said and flashed a grin. "He hates Butler. Says they don't run their program the right way."

Kevin was high-fiving himself inside, trying to stifle it. "IU, huh?" he managed to say.

"Yeah. Never been much of a hoops fan myself." Jeremiah shrugged. "I do remember seeing you, though. Everyone here remembers you."

Kevin gave him a nod. "Good to hear."

A carload of teens drove by.

Jeremiah watched it pass the Quick-Mart and head south. He spoke, "You *are* right about something."

"What's that?"

"I do care."

A car door creaked open, then another. More people entered the store. All getting their convenience fix.

"I'm sure you do," Kevin replied. "Tell me what you think really happened here, Jeremiah."

"If I tell you some things…things you need to know…can you keep my name out of it?"

Ashley Tyler called Casey again Saturday, six days after her initial news.

"I just wanted to let you know that I was late, but it's okay now," she said. "We're fine. I think it was just stress—why I was late. You know, everything that's happened."

Casey exhaled and glanced around to make sure his mom was nowhere within earshot. "You're sure?"

"Yes, we're in the clear," she said. "I don't think you want the details."

"I'm glad you called to tell me."

"Casey, I…I didn't mean to jump to conclusions like that, then blow you off like I have this week. It's just… well this has never happened before. I'm sorry to scare you."

"It's okay."

Ashley was silent a moment. "There's something else I wanted to say. I'm not sure we should see each other any more. Or at least…cool it awhile."

"Yeah, I agree," Casey responded, a bit too quickly. "I mean, I understand." He felt a huge wave of relief and his mind was already elsewhere.

"Thanks."

"Ashley, I just want to tell you…I'm sorry."

She was quiet again.

"Hey, sorry for what? We're fine. There's nothing to be sorry for."

"Yes there is."

Velma Moorer saw her son staring at the newspaper at the gas station.

Almost like he was hypnotized by it.

She read the headline of the front-page story and *knew* something was wrong all over again.

Van. The lying. The fact that Tommie was almost certainly still hiding something.

She decided to call Chief Rix back.

As he drove toward the outskirts of town, Kevin caught a glimpse of something out of the corner of his eye. A bright color.

He turned the car around. He wanted to be sure.

Heading into town, the sign read:

Welcome to
JASONVILLE
"Gateway to Shakamak"

It had a brown background with yellow writing and lattice-work fencing beneath the sign. Kevin drove past slowly, then craned his neck.

On the reverse side of the sign he read:

HURRY
BACK

Kevin did a U-turn and pulled the car to the side of the road. He checked the rearview mirror. No one was behind him.

He'd been right.

There it was under the message. In full Technicolor glory. A pink paintball splatter.

He was almost certain it hadn't been there before.

Tommie thought about all the commotion when he'd gotten back from the lake that night. How scared he had been, how afraid of getting in trouble, the vows he'd made to himself.

He'd picked a bad night to go out—maybe the worst one in Jasonville history—but it wasn't fair. No one had to know everything.

Why had his mom driven him to the cop shop again?

But there she was, turning off the car, fixing determined eyes on him.

"Mom, no."

"Just try it one more time, honey."

Kevin pulled up to the entrance of Shakamak State Park. He'd thought from his first day in town that he wanted to see this place, but it had been on the backburner till now.

On the drive out, he'd listened to a voicemail from O'Malley. "So far we're the only paper asking these questions," O'Malley had said with restrained excitement. "Pull it off, and we'll have the entire state hooked. I knew it was a good move keeping you there. Just move quick."

Kevin smiled. His boss's way of asking for more.

Another installment beckoned. He could picture it in his head. This could be the one. Soon, he would go to the Jasonville police for the final piece of the puzzle. He just needed some time to process what Jeremiah had told him.

"Hi," the toll lady said.

"I'm not from around here. People tell me this is worth seeing."

"Yes. Five dollars to come in, please."

She took his ten and gave him change. "There you go."

"Does this close at night?" he asked.

"Not if you're camping."

He pointed. "So would this gate be closed?"

"I think so. It's supposed to be."

"Really?"

"Yes, I mean, I never work that particular shift. But that's what they tell me."

"Interesting." He put his change away.

CASEY HUNG UP THE PHONE AND BURIED HIS FACE IN HIS HANDS.

His mother walked by. "What was that all about?" she asked, concern in her voice.

"Nothing. Just a girl."

"You seem upset."

"No." He smiled. "It's not that. I just…I need to get out of here for a while. Maybe go for a walk."

"Okay, dear."

"I might stop by and see if Mark's home. I shouldn't be gone long."

thirty-two

TOMMIE MOORER SAT ACROSS THE TABLE FROM BERTRAND RIX.

Even at the ripe young age of twelve, the boy had an alternative look in the works. Rix tried to make contact with the kid's dark brown eyes, but they darted around the room nervously. Tommie had high cheekbones and a long mop-top seventies haircut. He sported a stonewashed denim jacket that probably had an inside pocket destined for a cigarette pack, or maybe a cell phone.

Rix attempted a brief smile. Tommie finally gazed back. Rix folded his hands on the table.

"Tommie, I notice in your statement to Agent Zane that you said the person you saw at Lake Lenape was wearing a mask."

"Yeah," the kid said.

"But then later you refer to the person as a *guy*."

"Yeah."

"Why?"

A pause.

"I just assumed."

"Right, okay then. May I ask why? Did you see anything that would specifically suggest the individual was male?"

Tommie looked away.

The door opened. For a second Rix thought the kid might try to bolt.

Lorraine stood in the doorway, motioning for Rix to step out.

"Huggins with Terre Haute PD's on the line. Says he's got something for you."

Rix glanced back at the kid. "Can it wait?"

"He says we're probably gonna want to come up there, but he wanted to talk to you first."

"That right?"

"It's about"—Lorraine eyed the kid—"this."

"I'll call him soon as I'm done."

"Okay, Chief." She handed Rix an envelope and closed the door.

Rix decided it was now or never. He remained standing. "Now Tommie, I could really use your help here." He stepped closer and pulled back his shirt, revealing the carve marks along his shoulder. "That night you were out at Lenape, *this* is what happened to me out at the graveyard."

The kid winced.

Which was good, Rix knew, if he didn't overplay it.

Rix waited a moment before releasing his shirt. "Well, what if I told you that, unlike Agent Zane, I actually did some checking…and I *know* your brother didn't have anything to do with the Jasonville murders? In fact, he wasn't anywhere near here on the night in question."

Rix thought Tommie perked up a bit, then tried to rein himself in. "Now, I *believe* you when you say you rode out to Lenape alone. I believe you when you say you simply borrow your uncle's moped from time to time. It's not even an issue.

"Understand this: Your brother, Van, isn't going to have any problems with me. Neither are you, Tommie—I promise you that—if you'll just shoot straight with me.

"Now." Rix pulled a book from the envelope and slid it across the table. "I have the feeling you're about to become a star witness, if you're up to the challenge."

The Jasonville High School Annual came to a perfect stop right in front of Tommie.

"Whaddya say we get started?"

Tommie thought hard about what the cop had said to him. He tried to picture Van in the room, giving him the nod to go ahead and spill it. He thought about his mother and how tired he was of disappointing her.

Then he thought about the picture in the newspaper. He thought about the truth.

And Tommie decided, right then and there, to come clean.

He would tell the cop about seeing one of Van's old friends out at the lake, unmasked, throwing things into the water late that night.

He would tell about being terrified—though he'd really wanted to be the bravest kid in seventh grade.

He would tell everything.

The sign outside the graveyard declared "No parking after dark."

Kevin smiled. The word "No" was italicized and in red letters. He headed in, weaving through the headstones.

When he found the lone mausoleum known as Tyre's Tomb, he stopped and took some mental notes.

Then he got an idea.

He knew it would take some persuading. Some key players would have to be on board. But he thought he could pull it off.

It was time.

He scanned the cemetery again. *Yeah, I'm coming for you and your buddies, Red Mask. You just don't know it yet.*

thirty-three

Danny Capill and Mark Craver sat in Danny's red Mustang, which was parked in front of Mark's house.

"Hey, lemme show you something," said Danny.

"Nah, I've seen you nude before," Mark replied.

"I'm serious." Danny stared back, emotionless. "It's time."

"O…kay," said Mark.

Danny got out, motioning for Mark to follow, and unlocked the car's trunk. It popped open and Mark saw a black garbage bag, wrapped up in duct tape around a long, thin object.

Danny handed it to Mark. "Check this out."

Mark hesitated. "Dude, what the—?"

"Just unwrap it. Carefully."

Mark obeyed.

He pulled the tape off and threw the wad in the trunk. Then he slid the plastic down.

There, in broad daylight, was a machete.

Its blade stained.

Burgundy.

They eyed each other.

"This isn't…tell me this isn't, Danny."

Danny grinned, almost imperceptibly, then gave a nod.

Mark quickly pulled the bag back over the blade and threw it back in the trunk. "No!" He stepped back.

Danny shrugged slightly.

Mark scanned the neighborhood. He lowered his voice

and spoke through gritted teeth, "Why the hell isn't *that* at the bottom of Lake Lenape?"

Danny made a face of mocking concern. "Mark—"

"With the rest of them!"

"Chill yourself *out*," said Danny.

"No."

"Mark, Mark, Mark."

"Shut up. Just shut the hell up!" Mark stepped off the curb like he was walking away but then stopped. He put his hands in his hair. "Ohhh..." Mark shook his head, "you goddam idiot!"

"Calm down," said Danny. "Don't be a pansyass."

"Oh...okay. Yeah that's just—okay, answer me this: What the hell is that doing in your trunk?"

"Look, it—"

"We agreed, you sick bastard! We all agreed."

"I—"

"Should have made sure it ended up forty feet *under*, in the muck at the bottom of Lenape. *With everyone else's.*"

"Look, I couldn't get out there. My parents were up and my mom was watching me like a hawk. Then there were all the sirens and the pandemonium."

"That's a *crock*. You were supposed to go straight there."

"Look man, I'm sorry. Just cool off a minute. No one's going to find out." Danny grabbed Mark by the shoulder and pulled him closer. He looked around. "No one's watching. No one. See? It doesn't matter. Everyone *knows* Cameron did it."

"What about that reporter?" asked Mark. "His paper's been saying that people think Cam might not have acted alone."

"That'll die off. They're still going to prosecute Cameron for all the murders. The reporter will get bored here and leave, just like the rest of them."

"Your cornfield idea backfired," said Mark. "He didn't leave."

"Hey, don't be pointing fingers at me," Danny replied. "You knew there was going to be some heat. If he causes any more trouble, we'll come up with another way to deal with it."

Mark flinched. "What are you saying?"

"All part of the game," said Danny. "*Think*, Mark. You know they'll never be able to match everything up. *You know it.*"

Mark grew quiet. "You killed Trisha, and you're fine lettin' Cam go down for it."

"Don't get all righteous on me. I may puke." Danny pulled out a cigarette and lit up. Then he let out a breath and shrugged at Mark. "What about you?"

Mark pointed. "Man, you killed *Trisha*, and kept the knife as a souvenir!"

"Should we talk about a certain tease cheerleader who still walks and talks like life's as sweet as an ice cream sundae?"

"I didn't—"

"While some other sweetheart we didn't agree on is in the grave?"

"Hey, I didn't *lie* to everyone."

"No, you just killed the wrong girl."

"This isn't about me," Mark declared. "There's no way I could've known Meghan had a friend over—one who looked just like her from behind."

"And yet you're perfectly content to bag on me?" said Danny.

"You never said a single word about Trisha. We would've never agreed to you doin' Trisha."

"Man, quit saying her name like you're all sentimental for her or something. Just let it—"

"She was Neal's girl. Neal was a part of the Order."

"Spare me."

"He was our friend."

"No, he wasn't."

"He was *my* friend."

For a second Danny looked subdued, uncertain. Finally he spoke, "I probably did him a favor."

Mark scoffed, "*Yeah*, you forgot to tell Neal that."

"Craver, c'mon."

"Unbelievable, Danny," said Mark. "Just unbelievable."

"Let it slide. You know you will."

"Yeah, we're not even supposed to be *talking* about this. We agreed. Not until school's out."

"Talking," Danny chided, "or doing other things."

"Yeah, and what the hell was that the other day at Trisha's house?" asked Mark. "I don't care if you want to keep tabs on it. But goin' solo and messin' with a cop like that…reckless."

Danny smiled. "The *lady* cop."

"Exactly, man," Mark shook his head, "that's your problem. You need to stop playing it for thrills, thinking you're the boogeyman."

Danny took a puff of his cigarette. "Please."

"What if someone finds out about you messin' with that girl up at the sports store in Terre Haute? They'll put two and two together."

Danny didn't reply for a moment. "Weren't you the one who was always saying you wanted to do something big?"

"Well getting yourself noticed all across the county isn't what I had in mind." Mark glanced at the black bag. "You're pushing it, man. Too far."

"Yeah, gotcha." Danny slammed the trunk down.

And that's when they saw Casey Wood standing just a few feet away.

Mark's jaw dropped.

Danny got out his keys, took a step toward the driver side, then stopped. "Hello, Casey," he said.

The three of them exchanged tense stares.

"Uh, hey man, how long you been standing there?" Mark asked.

"Tell me…" Casey began, "tell me I didn't hear what I just heard."

"You didn't hear shit," said Danny. He put the keys in his pocket and stepped forward.

Mark was frozen.

"You killed Trisha," said Casey.

"Nah," said Danny, who kept coming forward. He flicked his cigarette to the ground.

"It wasn't Cameron. It was *you*."

Danny stood an inch from Casey's face.

"Casey, it's not what you think," Mark pleaded.

Casey ignored him. "So what's in the trunk, Danny?"

"Sure you wanna go there, Wood?" Danny hissed.

Casey glanced at Mark. "What's at the bottom of Lake Lenape?"

Mark looked sick. "Casey, please."

"Weapons, maybe? Whose?"

Danny shrugged.

"*Who?* Who all did this?"

"Casey, let's talk somewhere else," Mark stammered.

Casey's voice rose. "Who!"

"Cameron," said Mark.

"Lies."

"C'mon, Wood," said Danny. "This is Order business. You know how it is. Let's have a debriefing somewhere private."

"No, I don't know how it is. And killing people *isn't* Order business."

"C'mon Wood, give it up. No one killed anyone."

Casey pointed at Danny and looked at Mark. "He killed Trisha, didn't he?"

Mark answered without answering.

Danny stared into Casey's eyes. "Now you know I wouldn't have hurt Neal's girlfriend."

Casey clenched his jaw.

"But one thing we can agree on," Danny continued. "She's dead." He leaned even closer and Casey could smell his cigarette-smoke breath. "Dead fucking red."

Their eyes met and held, and that's when Casey saw the darkness there. Danny's eyes were the blackest Casey had ever seen. A chill blew over him, and everything made a sickening sort of sense.

He remembered the look on Hope's face, and the sinking feeling in his heart when he'd heard about Cameron. The downfall of the Order. The shattering of lives, friendships. Now he knew everything had begun here, right here behind these eyes.

Danny smiled.

Casey felt like he'd been knocked to his knees. His skin crawled. He could sense it—the dark place Danny had drawn from. Casey knew that Danny had manipulated them all. The truth was ugly, so incredibly ugly.

Casey scowled back. Danny seemed to be daring him to do something.

Dead fucking red...

Casey knew Danny could tear him apart. Danny was taller and outweighed him by a good twenty-five pounds.

And he was a killer.

The *leader* of the killers.

Survival instinct told Casey to walk away. That the Order could remain. That he could fake his way through their friendship for another year or two, and then the guys would go their separate ways in life. Mark would probably trust him. Mark could convince Danny enough was enough.

Danny was still sneering.

Then something happened in Casey that he had little control over. Slowly, very carefully, he brought his fingers together until his hand formed a fist.

Danny didn't notice.

Time felt like it was unfolding in slow motion. Casey

squeezed his hand tight and kneaded his clenched fingers against his palm.

Danny's black eyes narrowed.

Casey gritted his teeth.

Dead fucking red…

He threw the punch, as hard and as fast as he could, squarely at Danny's jaw.

"No!" yelled Mark.

The punch connected dead-on. Danny groaned and stumbled back.

Casey followed through, and for a second he thought Danny would go down. He waited for a reaction.

Mark rushed forward. "You guys, don't!" He looked nervously around.

Danny held his jaw. He let out another groan, then regained his balance.

Mark stood awkwardly, facing them.

Casey glanced at Mark, then back at Danny. He wanted to say something, but couldn't.

Danny let go of his jaw and glared at Casey.

Danny's face was demonic hatred, pure venom. Casey had never seen anything like it in his life.

Mark held up his palms and stepped forward. "Danny, please."

"Shut up, Craver," ordered Danny, his voice cold, raspy. He stared in shock at Casey, and for the tiniest moment looked hurt.

And then Casey saw something else in Danny's face, something that would haunt him forever—a glimpse of the Danny he was once friends with. The Danny who could be cool, who'd once stood up for Casey against a couple of jocks from Linton.

It didn't last long.

Danny ripped his keys out. He took a step back and spoke with strained indifference, "Like I said, I didn't kill Trisha. Or anyone. Talk to Cam."

Mark stood, frozen and wide-eyed.

Danny walked to his car, got in, and drove away.

Mark and Casey stood next to each other on the curb in stunned silence.

"Dude, I can't believe you hauled off and belted him," said Mark.

There was a pause.

"It doesn't end with him driving off, does it?" said Casey.

Mark squirmed, said nothing.

Casey finally broke the silence. "Who?"

"Whaddya mean?"

"You, Mark," Casey jabbed his finger in Mark's chest. "Beth Simmons, Geena Wolford, Claire Jordan, Karen Gothman, Hope Redmond. *Who?*"

Mark got very quiet, as if digging for some inner resolve.

Finally he spoke, in a voice that sounded a bit off, almost not his own. "Karen."

Casey shook his head and stared at his childhood pal. His eyes started welling up. "My God, Mark."

"Casey, I—"

"How could you go along with Danny on something like that? *How could you possibly—?*"

"C'mon, man!" Mark said, the intensity in his voice unnerving, "You hated her. We all talked about it."

"Talked!" Casey cut in. "It was just talk, Mark. *Talk!*"

"You act so damn innocent," Mark responded.

"I had no idea you guys would do something like this and you know it. What? You think you were doing me some *favor* killing Karen?"

Mark looked hauntingly toward his house, was silent.

"I didn't mean to kill her," he said finally.

"What?"

"Meghan, Casey. Meghan Reed. I thought she was Meghan."

Casey shook his head again. "Oh!" He stepped away,

then spun all the way around. He got up in Mark's face. "Tell me what difference *that* makes, Mark? *What's wrong with you!* She's a human being!"

Mark's eyes were glazed over now, too. He didn't respond.

"Who else?" said Casey.

"I...I can't."

"Did Danny stab Hope?"

"No." Mark looked away.

"Mark?"

"That's the one piece the cops have right."

Casey paused a moment and let Mark's words sink in.

"Cameron didn't kill anyone, did he?"

"No," Mark replied, "just tried to with Hope and the cop."

"Oh that's just wonderful," said Casey.

"The cop wasn't part of the plan, " said Mark. "Neither was Hope."

"Then why?" Casey demanded, cringing. "Why Hope?"

"Cam was after Ashley that night." Mark sniffed hard. "But someone you know was *busy* with her, Casey."

Casey's mouth fell open.

"Cam just moved on to the next girl. We'd talked about doing that. Hope was in the wrong place at the wrong time. Didn't really turn out well."

Casey shook his head, his mouth still open.

Mark looked at him wryly. "Hey, don't ask questions, my friend, if you aren't ready for the answers."

They both stared toward Mark's house.

Though he fought it, a tear rolled down Casey's cheek.

Casey spoke, almost in a whisper, "You and Danny didn't kill those other girls, did you?"

Mark didn't blink. "No."

"Eric took you spearfishing once, didn't he?"

Mark hesitated. "Yeah."

"Where's Eric's spear these days?"

Mark looked at him like the answer was obvious. "Gone."

"Lenape?"

Mark recoiled. "How did you...?"

Casey exhaled slowly. "Eric killed Geena, didn't he?"

"Yes."

"And Beth?"

"Eric also."

"*Unbelievable.* Who killed Claire? Eric or Danny? Or Jeremiah?"

Mark whispered. "Eric. It was Eric again. He wanted to do more than anyone. Jeremiah didn't have anything to do with it."

"Why did you guys go off on your own like that? How could you *kill people*?"

"Just cool off, man," said Mark.

"And Danny killing Trisha...were you fine with that?"

"No. Danny said he was gonna do Beth. I think he and Eric worked out some other plan on the side. Almost none of it went down like we planned."

"Like what it did to Neal for instance?"

"Don't..."

"You couldn't take it when he broke down at the lake, could you?"

"Shut up," said Mark.

"How could you do that to him? And those families? This town? How could the four of you trash the *Order*?"

"We only got together the guys we knew were serious, Casey. We knew everyone wouldn't do it. We knew when to quit."

"Oh, did you?" Casey shook his head. "Unbelievable, Mark, what the hell happened to you?"

Mark didn't reply.

"Why would you ever think of actually *trying to kill* Meghan?"

"We thought we should switch things around, so no one could add it all up," Mark said. "I got Meghan. Eric's idea, I think."

"And you guys are just gonna let Cameron take the fall for everything?"

"Look, we all agreed. We agreed that if someone got caught somehow, nobody would say a word. The cops will never be able to match everything up, unless one of us talks. It's simply not possible. We took the stuff up to Shakamak State Park and threw it in the lake. We knew if it ever went to a trial, a jury would probably just get confused trying to connect the dots. Lots of idiots out there. Cameron knew the deal. I think he'll hold to it. I don't expect you to understand."

Casey almost laughed. "That's about the only thing you've said that actually makes sense."

"You know, I would have thought you, of all people, *might* get it a little. You talk a good game, you're into all the movies, our discussions, the scenarios, but what? You still don't understand?"

"*No.*"

Mark spoke with urgency, "When you heard about the murders, the paintball mask, you...you had to know *something.*"

"Cameron's all I knew. Thought I knew."

"C'mon."

"Enough! Mark, I don't know you—or the guy who'd cross that line. *I never—*"

"Listen to me, Casey. Cam's going away. He stabbed a cop. They're coming down hard on him for that, no matter what. We made a pact for if something like this happened. There's no use everyone going away. Danny just got a scholarship to Indiana State. And man...I'm still a junior in high school. So are you. We've got our lives ahead of us. We're still a part of the Order."

"What about those girls' lives?"

"*Come on*, Casey! It's not like we're serial killers or

something. The world will still go on like it always has. Jasonville will heal. In six months half of us will be out of here. It won't matter."

"You don't really believe that, do you?"

"What are you talking about?"

"You're afraid."

"No," said Mark. "I'm not."

"You're not afraid of Danny?"

"No."

"Of Eric?"

Mark was quiet.

"He's not right anymore, is he?" said Casey.

Mark couldn't look at him. "He wants to plan more stuff...weird stuff. The three of us together. But it's not gonna happen. Danny's going to deal with it."

"Yeah, I can see how well Danny's dealing with things."

"Look man, I just...I can't go back," said Mark. "Forget I ever told you anything."

Casey grabbed him. "What about Neal? What about his future! *Their* futures!"

"Stop." Mark now wore a horrified expression on his face. "I...I'm sorry. I didn't want that to happen. I can't change it. Just forget I ever told you anything." He tried to pull away.

Casey let go and stared at his old friend. "When did you change so much, Mark? I didn't notice it happening."

"We're still friends."

"Are we?"

Mark didn't answer. He took a few steps toward the house and paused. A moment later he turned back and faced Casey.

"Remember when you fell off my roof?"

Casey smiled slightly. "Yes. I've never been in so much pain."

Mark laughed, suddenly transformed. "You couldn't breathe or talk. I felt so guilty. Had to help you. No, save you.

I still can't believe you let me drag your ass all the way from where you fell, through the yard, and inside to our couch."

Casey laughed. "I thought I was going to die going up your porch steps."

"Yeah, man. Good times," said Mark.

Their eyes met.

Casey remembered playing kickball together on the playground…sneaking into the girls' bathroom and letting a garter snake loose…cheering Mark on while he fought Damon Norton at summer camp…listening anxiously while Mark explained how to ask the opposite sex out on a date…sharing their first beer…chasing girls all over Jasonville.

That was one Mark. The other had slashed Karen Gothman's throat and left her to die.

Casey's face held still, but tears came racing down his cheeks.

"I'm sorry," whispered Mark, as if reading his thoughts. "You…you just can't let me rot away in a jail cell."

Mark turned and walked to his front door. He went in, and the screen door smacked back violently, then came to a rest.

A car drove by. Birds chirped from somewhere in the distance.

Casey stood silently and stared ahead at nothing in particular.

thirty-four

ERIC VATHENS HEADED OUT FOR A SUB. HE WAS SURPRISED TO FIND a note on his truck, lodged between the windshield and the wiper blade.

He glanced around at the neighbors' houses and up the street. He saw nothing. He opened the note and read:

> I SAW YOU THAT NIGHT.
>
> YOU DID SOMETHING BAD.
> NOW YOU'RE LETTING YOUR FRIEND
> TAKE THE RAP.
>
> MEET ME AT TYRE'S TOMB <u>TONIGHT</u>,
> JUST BEFORE THE SUN GOES DOWN.
>
> OR I GO STRAIGHT TO THE POLICE.

He opened his mouth to say the word "What?" but nothing came out.

Something was horribly wrong. There was no way anyone saw *him* that night.

So how did somebody know?

Eric felt something he wasn't used to. Fear.

He looked up to the sky, toward the west, and saw the sun was making its descent. He had maybe half an hour to decide what to do.

H<small>E</small> <small>WATCHED, HIDDEN OUT OF NORMAL VIEW, AS</small> E<small>RIC MADE HIS</small> way through the rows of graves and stopped right in front of the mausoleum. The Indiana sunset was just beginning to the west, and the fading rays formed a dim backdrop of light behind Tyre's Tomb.

All was quiet.

Eric didn't like the silence. He wanted to get this over with. He cast nervous glances to his sides and behind him.

"Okay, I'm here!" he shouted at the surrounding gravestones.

Kevin walked out from behind a large heart-shaped headstone to the right of Tyre's Tomb, carrying a black duffel bag.

"Hey there Eric, buddy."

Eric turned to face him, trying to understand, "You."

"I see you've trimmed your moustache some," Kevin said, "Looks a little skinny."

"*You*," Eric repeated, shaking his head.

"Yes, it's me. But I must tell you, I'm not alone." Kevin reached into the bag. "Look who I brought." He pulled out a stuffed pair of jeans. "Remember me, I'm your fantasy girl's legs."

Eric's face froze. "You..." His mind raced and he struggled for words. "You were in my room?"

Kevin played dumb. "Why would you say that?"

"You were digging around in my *closet*?"

Kevin jiggled his prop a little. "Maybe there's another explanation."

"That note you left me was bogus, wasn't it?" Eric glared. "Clever. But that doesn't prove squat."

"It is rather curious, though, ain't it?"

"Maybe to some desperate asshole."

Kevin looked Eric in the eyes. He could tell the kid was struggling to maintain the tough guy pose.

"You know, I think I'll keep these." Kevin started to cram the stuffed jeans back into his bag.

"I'm just about sick of you," Eric hissed.

"Sorry to hear that," Kevin replied. "You know what I'm sick of? This whole charade about Cameron Ford."

Eric flinched.

Kevin held up the bag. "Heyya Eric, what'd ya do with my torso? Did you throw that in Lake Lenape, too?"

Eric's eyes registered total shock and his mouth gaped open. He regained control. "Don't know *what* you're talking about. Have your reporting skills always sucked this bad?"

"Why would someone have seen you ditching things in Lake Lenape the night your pal Cameron Ford got arrested for killing all those girls?"

"No way," said Eric.

"Heard something in the bushes that night, didn't you?"

"What?" Eric started shifting his weight from one leg to the other, then back.

Kevin continued. "Just a little noise, some rustling that worried you. You'd probably forgotten all about it." Kevin dropped the bag on the ground in between them. "Till *now.*"

Eric offered no reply.

A crow cawed in the distance.

"Planning more murders?" Kevin goaded.

"No," said Eric, then gave Kevin a look that said *maybe just one more.*

"See, here's the biggest mistake you made that night, Eric. You searched around a little when you heard the noise, after you'd done your dirty work. But what you probably didn't know was that you should have been searching for someone small—like, for instance, *a kid.*"

Eric stood frozen, mouth open.

Kevin snapped his fingers.

Chief Rix stepped out from behind the big heart-shaped headstone.

TOMMIE STARED THROUGH THE FANCY BINOCULARS FROM THE outskirts of Lebanon Cemetery. "Yeah," he said, "that's him."

He handed the binoculars back to Agent Zane. "These are nice."

"Good work," Agent Zane replied. He turned to Agent Jergens. "Okay, let 'em know we got an ID."

Agent Jergens nodded and spoke into his radio. "You're good to go. We'll swing by for a final visual conf' once he's cuffed. *Out*."

"All right, let's go," said Agent Zane.

Tommie asked, "Shouldn't you guys like thank me or something?"

"Come with us," Agent Zane replied, motioning toward the car.

Before they got in, Agent Jergens leaned down and spoke in Tommie's ear. "That means thanks."

ERIC'S EYES BOUNCED BACK AND FORTH FROM KEVIN TO RIX. His jaw was tight.

Kevin said, "Oh, hey Chief. You just get here? Eric Vathens and I have been talking, and…well…Eric, I think you should pick up the story from here."

"*No*." Eric panicked and turned to run.

"FREEZE!" boomed Rix.

Deputy Lorraine Barrett appeared, blocking Eric's path, hand on her gun. "Like your life depended on it."

Eric did as he was told.

"Thank you, Mr. Gibson," said Rix. He stepped forward and cuffed Eric, then led him away.

"My pleasure," said Kevin. He followed.

Deputy Barrett read Eric his rights as they escorted him from the cemetery. Eric kept insisting he wasn't out at Lake Lenape that night.

When they reached the police cruiser, Tommie and the agents were standing there waiting.

"Yes, that's him," Tommie offered without hesitation. "I'm sure."

Agents Zane and Jergens nodded.

Eric stared at Tommie. "So *you* were in those damn weeds."

Tommie nodded. "That's right."

"You're *so* lucky."

Tommie didn't reply.

"All right, let's go," said Rix. "This place makes my shoulder hurt."

Eric turned as Deputy Barrett placed him into the car. Over his shoulder he sneered, "I'll say hi to your brother, kid."

Kevin waited for a reaction, surprised at the audacity.

"Shut up," said Tommie.

thirty-five

Cameron Ford woke up and shuddered.

Another bad dream.

He buried his face in his hands.

He wished he could talk to someone. Anyone. Just a single soul other than himself.

He sat up and stared out beyond the bars. Somewhere, outside in the night, was his freedom. Through the locked cell door, down the corridor maybe seventy paces, then to another locked door, then right and another fifty footsteps, then through the main entrance.

It lived and breathed on the other side, without him. The freedom he'd taken from himself.

He thought of Chaplain Ashton.

Cameron knew in his soul that there was another form of freedom. He wanted to find it.

He felt he understood now. Somehow he understood the words. He understood the cries, too. As much as possible.

But the lies, the lies more than anything, haunted him.

The guilt.

Cause and effect.

He looked over at the book, lying on the floor of his cell, right where he'd dropped it.

Cameron turned and gazed down the hall.

Funny thing, he'd hated the light when they'd first put him in there. Especially his first few nights. He'd missed his real bed at home terribly. And he'd wondered how he would

ever sleep in jail: *Why wouldn't they just turn off the lights?*
Cameron shook his head at the memory.

Now the light seemed different. Needed, maybe. There for a reason.

He picked up the book.

Cameron read through the pamphlet and list the chaplain had left for him. He flipped through the book for several minutes, stopping carefully and reading, the turning pages the only sound in the cell block.

He realized something.

He was by himself in the cell. But he wasn't alone.

Cameron's eyes watered.

The chaplain had written a prayer for him.

He closed his eyes and breathed deep. He exhaled and took another deep breath.

Cameron knew what had to happen, the step he had to take. Alone.

But then again he wasn't alone.

He blinked at the thought and drops hit the pages.

Somewhere out there was freedom. Truth.

And somehow it was right there with him, standing one step away, extending its hand.

He sniffed and wiped away at one eye, then the next. He gazed out in the hallway and almost smiled.

Cameron bowed his head.

thirty-six

CASEY PULLED INTO THE PARKING LOT OF GREENE COUNTY General. He'd heard she was finally ready to be released.

He went to turn off the car and glanced at the clock. He'd made the ten-and-a-half-mile drive from Jasonville to Linton in seven minutes flat. He looked up.

There was a young woman in a wheelchair just outside the hospital.

He got out of the car. It was a beautiful day out. He took off his sunglasses and stared, then was sure.

Hope.

Casey smiled.

Why was she just sitting there?

He walked hurriedly.

She turned and saw him. She smiled. Gingerly, she rose and took a step his direction.

Man, she was beautiful. Even though she was a little weak and unkempt, she looked magical in the sunlight.

He laughed and almost ran.

"Hope!"

"Casey! How did you know?"

"It's so fantastic to see you."

She reached for him and they embraced.

"Casey…thanks for coming all the way up here." Hope said, her voice quivering. She was silent a moment. "Thank you for…before."

He held her gently. She might have been crying.

Hope's mother emerged from the door with handfuls of belongings. "Honey, I found them, we can—" she stopped and stared. "*Oh.*"

Mrs. Redmond looked uncertain for a moment, then smiled.

Casey and Hope remained in their embrace.

"It's over now," he whispered. "I've made sure."

"I heard."

Casey nodded toward Mrs. Redmond.

Hope gripped him tighter.

epilogue

EXCERPT FROM KEVIN GIBSON,
WRITING IN THE *INDIANAPOLIS TRIBUNE*

JASONVILLE, Ind.—A massive blue water tower overlooking the town reads "Jasonville: Gateway to Shakamak," announcing the small community's proximity to a popular Indiana state park.

But also visible now are the names someone has spray-painted across the water tower in bright red letters "Trisha, Beth, Claire, Karen, Geena, Neal." The graffiti tribute is for Jasonville High students Trisha Geller, Beth Simmons, Claire Borden, Karen Gothman, Geena Wolford, and Neal Jordan.

Geller, Simmons, Borden, Gothman, and Wolford were all found slain last month, on a rainy Friday night that forever changed the face of this tiny Indiana community. Jordan, who had been dating Geller, committed suicide not long after the murders.

Another victim, student Hope Redmond, was hospitalized for over two weeks but is expected to make a full recovery from a brutal knife attack.

Meanwhile, four of the victims' classmates are sitting in jail, three charged with murder and conspiracy to commit murder, the fourth with attempted murder and conspiracy.

264 — JEFFREY LEEVER

In a place where deep woods and tall cornfields combine with a seemingly horror-film-inspired town name, this much is known: Life here may never be quite the same, and high school students Danny Capill, Eric Vathens, Mark Craver, and Cameron Ford are locked up, awaiting trial. Greene County Prosecutor and Congressional candidate Merrill Cross has announced the young men, ranging in age from 16 to 18, will be tried as adults—except for Cameron Ford.

Ford, according to Cross, was originally arrested and charged with all five murders, the stabbing of Redmond, and an attack on Jasonville Police Chief Bertrand Rix. But just as Ford—who participated in the conspiracy but did not kill anyone—was in the process of turning state's evidence, another student was also coming forward: Jasonville High junior Casey Wood.

What Wood revealed to authorities—a shocking tale of boys-next-door turned murderers, would ultimately rock the community—and set in motion a chain of events that would put three more of his friends, including his best friend, behind bars. Key prosecution testimony is also expected from a Jasonville seventh-grader and a waitress from Terre Haute when the cases go to trial next month.

In the meantime, Wood—the seventeen-year-old reluctant hero—has sparked a national conversation about movie violence and life imitating art. And perhaps more importantly, the story of Jasonville, and a group of seemingly normal small-town teens, has stirred deeper questions about truth, friendship, justice, and the moral conscience of America.

FIVE YEARS LATER

The gate opened and Cameron Ford walked through tentatively, unsure if the ground would give way beneath his feet.

Ten steps into his newly granted freedom, he saw the chaplain. Just as Miles Ashton had promised five-and-a-half years ago, he was there to greet Cameron upon his release.

"Ready for your coming-home party?"

"I'm ready for anything but *that*," Cameron said, pointing behind himself.

"Your mother and sister are waiting, been working almost nonstop for two days. They've put together quite the celebration."

Cameron smiled.

"You never know who might be there."

He nodded.

Chaplain Ashton patted him on the shoulder. "Okay, be honest now. Which fast food joint did you miss the most?"

Cameron's eyes felt watery. "I've been thinking about this and wanted to ask you something. How do you do it…what you do, I mean? What's your secret?"

Chaplain Ashton stared at him. "Interesting question." He flashed a gentle grin. "If I told you, it wouldn't be a secret."

The chaplain waited a beat.

"Actually, I'm not sure there's any *secret* involved. But if there is, you'll have to figure it out on your own."

Cameron gazed at him and smiled.

Chaplain Ashton spoke, "Another five years from now, if you still don't know, ask me again and I'll tell you."

"Deal."

They were almost to the chaplain's car.

Cameron took a deep breath of freedom's air and thanked God silently. He thought about redemption, the power of choices, and the little things he'd taken for granted—like hugging his mom and sister.

He was ready to heal some scars. And tonight when he went to sleep in his own bed, he would look forward to tomorrow.

JEFFREY LEEVER SERVES AS A COPYWRITER FOR A TOP KANSAS CITY advertising agency, and is a former press office staffer with the Colorado Governor's Office.

He also writes an online college football column, the *Scarlet Commentary*. Jeffrey's short story *Pre-emptive Measures* was adapted and performed as a play in Colorado last year.

He holds a degree in English with an emphasis in writing, and is a member of several professional writers' organizations. Jeffrey lives in Missouri, and is currently at work on his next novel.

His website is www.jeffreyleever.com.